Neil Munro's
ERCHIE

SEANACHAIDH
PUBLISHING LTD

14 William Street, Greenock PA15 1BT

First Published: 1931, Wm. Blackwood, Edinburgh.
Original Material: Seanachaidh Presentations Ltd., 1987
Design and Illustrations: Seanachaidh Presentations Ltd., 1987.
Printed 1987
Reprinted 1989
This printing Jan. 1990

ISBN: 0 948963 25 5

Cover Design by William Stewart.
Illustrations by Donald Ward.

Typeset by: S.B.S., Port Glasgow.
Printed by: Bell and Bain Ltd.,Glasgow.

CONTENTS

Other Titles By Seanachaidh Presentations Ltd:

Para Handy (Illustrated)
The Very Best of Para Handy (Twin Cassette)
Folklore of the Scots
Legends of the Clans
Giants of Loch Shiel and other Scottish Tales
The Fairy Mound and other Scottish Tales

The above titles are also available as STORY CASSETTES
For a full list of current titles, contact the Publisher

ERCHIE

I

INTRODUCTION TO AN ODD CHARACTER

On Sundays he is the beadle of our church; at other times he Waits. In his ecclesiastical character there is a solemn dignity about his deportment that compels most of us to call him Mr MacPherson. In his secular hours, when passing the fruit at a city banquet, or when at the close of the repast he sweeps away the fragments of the dinner-rolls, and whisperingly expresses in your left ear a fervent hope that, "ye've enjoyed your dinner," he is simply Erchie.

Once I forgot, deluded a moment into a Sunday train of thought by his reverent way of laying down a bottle of Pommery, and called him Mr MacPherson. He reproved me with a glance of his eye.

"There's nae Mr MacPhersons here," said he afterwards; "at whit ye might call the social board I'm jist Erchie, or whiles Easy-gaun Erchie wi' them that kens me langest. There's sae mony folks in this world don't like to hurt your feelings that if I was kent as Mr MacPherson on this kind o' job I wadna mak' enough to pay for starchin' my shirts."

I suppose Mr MacPherson has been snibbing-in preachers in St Kentigern's Kirk pulpit and then going for twenty minutes' sleep in the vestry since the Disruption; and the more privileged citizens of Glasgow during two or three generations of public dinners have experienced the kindly ministrations of Erchie, whose proud motto is "A flet fit but a warm hert." I think, however, I was the first to discover his long pent-up and precious strain of philosophy.

On Saturday nights, in his office as beadle of St Kentigern's he lights the furnaces that take the chill off the Sunday devotions. I found him stoking the kirk fires one Saturday, not very much like a beadle in appearance, and much less like a waiter. It was what, in England, they call the festive season.

"There's mair than guid preachin' wanted to keep a kirk gaun," said he; "if I was puttin' as muckle dross on my fires as the Doctor puts in his sermons, efter a Setterday at the gowf, ye wad see a bonny difference on the plate. But it's nae odds—a beadle gets sma' credit, though it's him that keeps the kirk tosh and warm, and jist

1

at that nice easy-osy temperature whaur even a gey cauldrife member o' the congregation can tak' his nap and no' let his lozenge slip doon his throat for chitterin' wi' the cauld."

There was a remarkably small congregation at St Kentigern's on the following day, and when the worthy beadle had locked the door after dismissal he joined me on the pavement,

"Man," he said, "it was a puir turn-oot yon—hardly worth puttin' on fires for. It's aye the wye; when I mak' the kirk a wee bit fancy, and jalouse there's shair to be twa pound ten in the plate, on comes a blash o' rain, and there's hardly whit wid pay for the starchin' o' the Doctor's bands.

"Christmas! They ca't Christmas, but I could gie anither name for't. I looked it up in the penny almanac, and it said, 'Keen frost; probably snow,' and I declare-to if I hadna nearly to soom frae the hoose.

"The almanacs is no' whit they used to be; the auld chaps that used to mak' them maun be deid.

"They used to could do't wi' the least wee bit touch, and tell ye in January whit kind o' day it wad be at Hallowe'en, besides lettin' ye ken the places whaur the Fair days and the 'ool-markets was, and when they were to tak' place—a' kind o' information that maist o' us that bocht the almanacs couldna sleep at nicht wantin'. I've seen me get up at three on a cauld winter's mornin' and strikin' a licht to turn up Orr's Penny Commercial and see whit day was the Fair at Dunse. I never was at Dunse in a' my days, and hae nae intention o' gaun, but it's a grand thing knowledge, and it's no' ill to cairry. It's like poetry—'The Star o' Rabbie Burns' and that kind o' thing— ye can aye be givin' it a ca' roond in your mind when ye hae naething better to dae.

"Oh, ay! A puir turn-oot the day for Kentigern's; that's the drawback o' a genteel congregation like oors—mair than half o' them's sufferin' frae Christmas turkey and puttin' the blame on the weather.

"The bubbly-jock is the symbol o' Scotland's decline and fa'; we maybe bate the English at Bannockburn, but noo they're haein' their revenge and underminin' oor constitution wi' the aid o' a bird that has neither a braw plumage nor a bonny sang, and costs mair than the price o' three or four ducks. England gave us her bubbly-jock and took oor barley-bree.

"But it's a' richt; Ne'erday's comin'; it's begun this year gey early, for I saw Duffy gaun up his close last nicht wi' his nose peeled."

'Am I gaun hame, or am I comin' frae't, can ye tell me?' says he, and he was carryin' something roond-shaped in his pocket-naipkin.'

"Whit's wrang wi' ye, puir cratur?" I says to him.

'I was struck wi' a sheet o' lichtnin',' says he, and by that I ken't he had been doon drinkin' at the Mull of Kintyre Vaults, and that the season o' peace on earth, guid-will to men was fairly started.

'MacPherson,' he says, wi' the tear at his e'e, 'I canna help it, but I'm a guid man.'

"Ye are that, Duffy," I says, "when ye're in your bed sleepin'; at ither times ye're like the rest o' us, and that's gey middlin'. Whit hae ye in the naipkin?"

"He gied a dazed look at it, and says, 'I'm no shair, but I think it's a curlin'-stane, and me maybe gaun to a bonspiel at Carsbreck.'

"He opened it oot, and found it was a wee, roond, red cheese."

'That's me, a' ower,' says he— a Christmas for the wife,' and I declare there was as much drink jaupin' in him as wad hae done for a water-shute.

"Scotland's last stand in the way o' national customs is bein' made at the Mull o' Kintyre Vaults, whaur the flet half-mutchkin, wrapped up in magenta tissue paper so that it'll look tidy, is retreatin' doggedly, and fechtin' every fit o' the way, before the invadin' English Christmas caird. Ten years ago the like o' you and me couldna prove to a freen' that we liked him fine unless we took him at this time o' the year into five or six public-hooses, leaned him up against the coonter, and grat on his dickie. Whit dae we dae noo? We send wee Jennie oot for a shilling box o' the year afore last's patterns in Christmas cairds, and show oor continued affection and esteem at the ha'penny postage rate.

"Instead o' takin' Duffy roon' the toon on Ne'erday, and hurtin' my heid wi' trying' to be jolly, I send him a Christmas caird, wi' the picture o' a hayfield on the ootside and 'Wishin' you the Old, Old Wish, Dear,' on the inside, and stay in the hoose till the thing blaws bye.

"The shilling box o' Christmas cairds is the great peacemaker; a gross or twa should hae been sent oot to Russia and Japan, and it wad hae stopped the war. Ye may hae thocht for a twelvemonth the MacTurks were a disgrace to the tenement, wi' their lassie learnin' the mandolin', and them haein' their gas cut off at the meter for no' payin' the last quarter; but let them send a comic caird to your

3

lassie—'Wee Wullie to Wee Jennie,' and they would get the len' o' your wife's best jeely-pan.

"No' but whit there's trouble wi' the Christmas caird. It's only when ye buy a shillin' box and sit doon wi' the wife and weans to consider wha ye'll send them to that ye fin' oot whit an awfu' lot o' freen's ye hae. A score o' shillin' boxes wadnae gae ower half the kizzens I hae, wi' my grandfaither belangin' to the Hielan's, so Jinnet an' me jist let's on to some o' them we're no sendin' ony cairds oot this year because it's no' the kin' o' society go ony langer. And ye have aye to keep pairt o' the box till Ne'erday to send to some o' the mair parteecular anes ye forgot a' thegither were freen's o' yours till they sent ye a caird.

"Anither fau't I hae to the Christmas cairds is that the writin' on them's generally fair rideeculous.

'May Christmas Day be Blythe and Gay, and bring your household Peace and Joy,' is on the only caird left ower to send to Mrs Maclure; and when ye're shearin' aff the selvedges o't to mak' it fit a wee envelope, ye canna but think that it's a droll message for a hoose wi' five weans lyin' ill wi' the whoopin'-cough, and the man cairryin' on the wye Maclure does.

'Old friends, old favourites, Joy be with you at this Season,' says the caird for the MacTurks, and ye canna but mind that every third week there's a row wi' Mrs MacTurk and your wife aboot the key o' the washin'-hoose and lettin' the boiler rust that bad a' the salts o' sorrel in the Apothecaries 'll no tak' the stains aff your shirts.

"Whit's wanted is a kin' o' slidin' scale o' sentiment on Christmas cairds, so that they'll taper doon frae a herty greetin' ye can truthfully send to a dacent auld freen' and the kind o' cool 'here's to ye!' suited for an acquaintance that borrowed five shillin's frae ye at the Term, and hasna much chance o' ever payin't back again.

"If it wasna for the Christmas cairds a lot o' us wad maybe never jalouse there was onything parteecular merry aboot the season. Every man that ye're owin' an accoont to sends it to ye then, thinkin' your hert's warm and your pouches rattlin'. On Christmas Day itsel' ye're aye expectin' something; ye canna richt tell whit it is, but there's ae thing certain—that it never comes. Jinnet, my wife, made a breenge for the door every time the post knocked on Thursday, and a' she had for't at the end o' the day was an ashet fu' o' whit she ca's valenteens, a' written on so that they'll no even dae for next year.

"I used to wonder whit the banks shut for at Christmas, but I ken noo; they're feart that their customers, cairried awa' wi' their feelin' o' guid-will to men, wad be makin' a rush on them to draw money for presents, and maybe create a panic.

"Sae far as I can judge there's been nae panic at the banks this year.

"Every Ne'erday for the past fifty years I hae made up my mind I was gaun to be a guid man," he went on. "It jist wants a start, they tell me that's tried it, and I'm no' that auld. Naething bates a trial.

"I'm gaun to begin at twelve o'clock on Hogmanay, and mak' a wee note o't in my penny diary, and put a knot in my hankie to keep me in mind. Maist o' us would be as guid's there's ony need for if we had naething else to think o'. It's like a man that's hen-taed—he could walk fine if he hadna a train to catch, or the rent to rin wi' at the last meenute, or somethin' else to bother him. I'm gey faur wrang if I dinna dae the trick this year, though.

"Oh! ay. I'm gaun to be a guid man. No' that awfu' guid that auld freen's 'll rin up a close to hide when they see me comin', but jist dacent–jist guid enough to please mysel', like Duffy's singin'. I'm no' makin' a breenge at the thing and sprainin' my leg ower't. I'm startin' canny till I get into the wye o't. Efter this, Erchie MacPherson's gaun to flype his ain socks and no' leave his claes reel-rall aboot the hoose at night for his wife Jinnet to lay oot richt in the mornin'. I've lost money by that up till noo, for there was aye bound to be an odd sixpence droppin' oot and me no' lookin'. I'm gaun to stop skliffin' wi' my feet; it's sair on the boots. I'm gaun to save preens by puttin' my collar stud in a bowl and a flet-iron on the top o't to keep it frae jinkin' under the chevalier and book-case when I'm sleepin'. I'm gaun to wear oot a' my auld waistcoats in the hoose. I'm——"

"My dear Erchie," I interrupted, "these seem very harmless reforms."

"Are they?" said he. "They'll dac to be gaun on wi' the noo, for I'm nae phenomena, I'm jist Nature, jist the Rale Oreeginal."

II

ERCHIE'S FLITTING

He came down the street in the gloaming on Tuesday night with a bird-cage in one hand and a potato-masher in the other, and I knew at once, by those symptoms, that Erchie was flitting.

"On the long trail, the old trail, the trail that is always new, Erchie?" said I, as he tried to push the handle of the masher as far up his coat sleeve as possible, and so divert attention from a utensil so ridiculously domestic and undignified.

"Oh, we're no' that bad!" said he. "Six times in the four-and-forty year. We've been thirty years in the hoose we're leavin' the morn, and I'm fair oot o' the wye o' flittin'. I micht as weel start the dancin' again."

"Thirty years! Your household gods plant a very firm foot, Erchie."

"Man, ay! If it wisna for Jinnet and her new fandangles, I wad nae mair think o' flittin' than o' buyin a balloon to mysel'; but ye ken women! They're aye gaun to be better aff onywhaur else than whaur they are. I ken different, but I havena time to mak' it plain to Jinnet."

On the following day I met Erchie taking the air in the neighbourhood of his new domicile, and smoking a very magnificent meerschaum pipe.

"I was presented wi' this pipe twenty years ago," said he, "by a man that went to California, and I lost it a week or twa efter that. It turned up at the flittin'. That's ane o' the advantages o' flittin's; ye find things ye havena seen for years."

"I hope the great trek came off all right, Erchie?"

"Oh, ay! no' that bad, considerin' we were sae much oot o' practice. It's no' sae serious when ye're only gaun roond the corner to the next street. I cairried a lot o' the mair particular wee things roond mysel' last nicht—the bird-cage and Gledstane's picture and the room vawzes and that sort o' thing—but at the hinder-end Jinnet made me tak' the maist o' them back again."

"Back again, Erchie?"

"Ay. She made oot that I had cairried ower sae muckle that the flittin' wad hae nae appearance on Duffy's cairt, and haein' her mind set on the two rakes, and a' the fancy things lying at the close-mooth o' the new hoose till the plain stuff was taken in, I had just to cairry back a guid part o' whit I took ower last nicht. It's a rale divert the pride o' women! But I'm thinkin' she's vex't for't the day, because yin o' the things I took back was a mirror, and it was broke in Duffy's cairt. It's a gey unlucky thing to break a lookin'-gless."

"A mere superstition, Erchie."

"Dod! I'm no' sae shair o' that. I kent a lookin'-gless broke at a flittin' afore this, and the man took to drink a year efter't, and has been that wye since."

"How came you to remove at all?"

"I wad never hae happened if I hadna gane to a sale and seen a coal-scuttle. It's a dangerous thing to introduce a new coal-scuttle into the bosom o' your family. This was ane o' thae coal-scuttles wi' a pentin' o' the Falls o' Clyde and Tillitudlem Castle on the lid. I got it for three-and-tuppence; but it cost me a guid dale mair than I bargained for. The wife was rale ta'en wi't, but efter a week or twa she made oot that it gar'd the auld room grate we had look shabby, and afore ye could say knife she had in a new grate wi' wally sides till't, and an ash-pan I couldna get spittin' on. Then the mantelpiece wanted a bed pawn on't to gie the grate a dacent look, and she pit on a plush yin. Ye wadna hinder her efter that to get plush-covered chairs instead o' the auld hair-cloth we got when we were mairried. Her mither's chist-o'-drawers didna gae very weel wi' the plush chairs, she found oot in a while efter that, and they were swapped wi' two pound for a chevalier and book-case, though the only books I hae in the hoose is the Family Bible, Buchan's 'Domestic Medicine,' and the 'Tales o' the Borders.' It wad hae been a' richt if things had gane nae further, but when she went to a sale hersel' and bought a Brussels carpet a yaird ower lang for the room, she made oot there was naethin' for't but to flit to a hoose wi' a bigger room. And a' that happened because a pented coal-scuttle took ma e'e."

"It's an old story, Erchie; 'c'est le premier pas que coûte,' as the French say."

"The French is the boys!" says Erchie, who never gives himself away. "Weel, we're flittin' onywye, and a bonny trauchle it is. I'll no' be able to find my razor for a week or twa."

"It's a costly process, and three flittin's are worse than a fire, they say."

"It's worse than that; it's worse than two Irish lodgers.

'It'll cost jist next to naethin', says Jinnet. 'Duffy 'll tak' ower the furniture in his lorry for freen'ship's sake, an' there's naethin' 'll need to be done to the new hoose.'

"But if ye ever flitted yersel', ye'll ken the funny wyes o' the waxcloth that's never cut the same wye in twa hooses; and I'll need to gey thrang at my tred for the next month or twa to pay for the odds and ends that Jinnet never thought o'.

"Duffy flitted us for naethin', but ye couldna but gie the man a dram. A flittin' dram's by-ordinar; ye daurna be scrimp wi't, or they'll break your delf for spite, and ye canna be ower free wi't either, or they'll break everything else oot o' fair guid-natur. I tried to dae the thing judeecious but I forgot to hide the bottle, and Duffy's heid man and his mate found it when I wasna there, and that's the wye the lookin'-gless was broken. Thae cairters divna ken their ain strength.

"It's a humblin' sicht your ain flittin' when ye see't on the tap o' a coal-lorry."

"Quite so, Erchie; chiffoniers are like a good many reputations— they look all right so long as you don't get seeing the back of them."

"And cairters hae nane o' the finer feelin's, I think. In spite o' a' that Jinnet could dae, they left the pots and pans a' efternoon on the pavement, and hurried the plush chairs up the stair at the first gae-aff. A thing like that's disheartenin' to ony weel-daein' woman.

'Hoots!,' says I to her, 'whit's the odds? There's naebody heedin' you nor your flittin',,'

'Are they no'?' said Jinnet, keekin' up at the front o' the new land. 'All the venetian blinds is doon, and I'll guarantee there's een behind them.'

"We werena half-an-oor in the new hoose when the woman on the same stairheid chappet at the door and tellt us it was oor week o' washin' oot the close. It wasna weel meant, but it did Jinnet a lot o' guid, for she was sittin in her braw new hoose greetin'."

"Greetin', Erchie? Why?"

"Ask that! Ye'll maybe ken better than I dae."

"Well, you have earned your evening pipe at least, Erchie," said I.

He knocked out its ashes on his palm with a sigh. "I hiv that! Man, it's a gey dauntenin' thing a flittin', efter a'. I've a flet fit, but a warm hert, and efter thirty years o' the auld hoose I was sweart to leave't. I brocht up a family in't, and I wish Jinnet's carpet had been a fit or two shorter, or that I had never seen yon coal-scuttle wi' the Falls o' Clyde and Tillitudlem Castle."

III
DEGENERATE DAYS

"The tred's done," said Erchie.

"What! beadling?" I asked him.

"Oh! there's naethin' wrang wi' beadlin'," said he; "there's nae up and doons there except to put the books on the pulpit desk, and they canna put ye aff the job if ye're no jist a fair wreck. I'm a' richt for the beadlin' as lang's I keep me health and had Jinnet to button my collar, and it's generally allo'ed—though maybe I shouldna say't mysel'—that I'm the kind o' don at it roond aboot Gleska. I michtna be, if I wasna gey carefu'. Efter waitin' at a Setterday nicht spree, I aye tak' care to gie the bell an extra fancy ca' or twa on the Sunday mornin' jist to save clash and mak' them ken MacPherson's there himsel', and no' some puir pick-up that never ca'd the handle o' a kirk bell in his life afore.

"There's no' a man gangs to oor kirk wi' better brushed boots than mysel', as Jinnet 'll tell ye, and if I hae ae gift mair than anither it's discretioncy. A beadle that's a waiter has to gae through life like the puir troot they caught in the Clyde the other day—wi' his mooth shut, and he's worse aff because he hasna ony gills—at least no' the kind ye pronounce that way.

"Beadlin's an art, jist like pentin' photograph pictures, or playin' the drum, and if it's no' in ye' naethin' 'll put it there. I whiles see wee skinamalink craturs dottin' up the passages in U.F. kirks carryin' the books as if they were M.C.'s at a dancin'-schule ball gaun to tack up the programme in front o' the band; they lack thon rale releegious glide; they havena the feet for't.

"Waitin' is whit I mean; it's fair done!

"When I began the tred forty-five year syne in the auld Saracen Heid Inn, a waiter was looked up to, and was well kent by the best folk in the toon, wha aye ca'd him by his first name when they wanted the pletform box o' cigaurs handed doon instand o' the Non Plus Ultras.

"Nooadays they stick a wally door-knob wi' a number on't in the lapelle o' his coat, and it's 'Hey, No.9, you wi' the flet feet, dae ye ca' this ham?'

"As if ye hadna been dacently christened and brocht up an honest faimily!

"In the auld days they didna drag a halflin callan' in frae Stra'ven, cut his nails wi' a hatchet, wash his face, put a dickie and a hired suit on him, and gie him the heave into a banquet-room, whaur he disna ken the difference between a finger-bowl and a box o' fuzuvian lichts.

"I was speakin' aboot that the ither nicht to Duffy, the coalman, and he says, 'Whit's the odds, MacPherson? Wha the bleezes couldna sling roon' blue-mange at the right time if he had the time-table, or the menu, or whitever ye ca't, to keep him richt?' 'Wha couldna sell coal,' said I, 'if he had the jaw for't? Man, Duffy,' says I, 'I never see ye openin' your mooth to roar coal up a close but I wonder whit wye there should be sae much talk in the Gleska Toon Cooncil aboot the want o' vacant spaces.'

"Duffy's failin'; there's nae doot o't. He has a hump on him wi' carryin' bags o' chape coal and dross up thae new, genteel, tiled stairs, and he let's on it's jist a knot in his gallowses, but I ken better. I'm as straucht as a wand mysel'—faith, I micht well be, for a' that I get to cairry hame frae ony o' the dinners nooadays. I've seen the day, when Blythswood Square and roond aboot it was a' the go, that it was coonted kind o' scrimp to let a waiter hame withoot a heel on him like yin o' thae Clyde steamers gaun oot o' Rothesay quay on a Fair Setturday.

"Noo they'll ripe your very hip pooches for fear ye may be takin' awa' a daud o' custard, or the toasted crumbs frae a dish o' pheasant.

"They needna' be sae awfu' feart, some o' them. I ken their dinners—cauld, clear, bane juice, wi' some string o' vermicilli in't; ling-fish hash; a spoonfu' o' red-currant jeely, wi' a piece o' mutton the size o' a domino in't, if ye had time to find it only ye're no' playin' kee-hoi; a game croquette that's jist a flaff o' windy paste; twa cheese straws; four green grapes, and a wee lend o' pair o' silver nut-crackers the wife o' the hoose got at her silver weddin'.

"Man! it's a rale divert! I see big, strong, healthy Bylies and members o' the Treds' Hoose and the Wine, Speerit, and Beer Tred risin' frae dinners like that, wi' their big, braw, gold watch-chains hingin' doon to their knees.

"As I tell Jinnet mony a time, it's women that hae fair ruined dinner-parties in oor generation. They tak' the measure o' the appetites o' mankind by their ain, which hae been a'thegether spoiled wi' efternoon tea, and they think a man can mak' up wi' music in the drawin'-room for whit he didna get at the dinner-table.

"I'm a temperate man mysel', and hae to be, me bein' a beadle, but I whiles wish we had back the auld days I hae read aboot, when a laddie was kept under the table to lowse the grauvats o' the gentlemen that fell under't, in case they should choke themsel's. Scotland was Scotland then!

"If they choked noo, in some places I've been in, it wad be wi' thirst.

"The last whisk o' the petticoat's no roon' the stair-landin' when the man o' the hoose puts the half o' his cigarette bye for again, and says, 'The ladies will be wonderin' if we've forgotten them,' and troosh a' the puir deluded craturs afore him up the stair into the drawin'-room where his wife Eliza's maskin' tea, and a lady wi' tousy hair's kittlin' the piano till its sair.

'Whit's your opinion about Tschaikovski?' I heard a wumman ask a Bylie at a dinner o' this sort the ither nicht.

'I never heard o' him,' said the Bylie, wi' a gant, 'but if he's in the proveesion tred, there'll be an awfu' run on his shop the morn's morn'.'

"Anither thing that has helped to spoil oor tred is the smokin' concerts. I tak' a draw o' the pipe mysel' whiles, but I never cared to mak' a meal o't. Noo and then when I'm no' very busy other ways I gie a hand at a smoker, and it mak's me that gled I got ower my growth afore the thing cam' into fashion; but it's gey sair on an auld man to hear 'Queen o' the Earth' five or six nichts in the week, and the man at the piano aye tryin' to guess the richt key, or to get done first, so that the company 'll no' rin awa' when he's no' lookin' withoot paying him his five shillin's.

"I've done the waitin' at a' kinds o' jobs in my time—Easy-gaun Erchie they ca' me sometimes in the tred—a flet fit but a warm hert; I've even handed roond seed-cake and a wee drap o' spirits at a burial, wi' a bereaved and mournfu' mainner that greatly consoled the weedow; but there's nae depths in the business so low as poo'in' corks for a smokin' concert. And the tips get smaller and smaller every ane I gang to. At first we used to get them in a schooner gless; then it cam' doon to a wee tumbler; and the last I was at I got the bawbees in an egg-cup."

IV
THE BURIAL OF BIG MACPHEE

Erchie looked pityingly at Big Macphee staggering down the street. "Puir sowl!" said he, "whit's the maitter wi' ye noo?"

Big Macphee looked up, and caught his questioner by the coat collar to steady himself. "Beer," said he; "jist beer. Plain beer, if ye want to ken. It's no' ham and eggs, I'll bate ye. Beer, beer, glorious beer; I'm shair I've perished three gallons this very day. Three gallons hiv I in me, I'll wager."

"Ye wad be far better to cairry it hame in a pail," said Erchie. "Man, I'm rale vexed to see a fine, big, smert chap like you gaun hame like this, takin' the breadth o' the street."

"Hiv I no' a richt to tak' the breadth o' the street if I want it?" said Big Macphee. "Am I no' a ratepayer? I hiv a ludger's vote, and I'm gaun to vote against Joe Chamberlain and the dear loaf."

"Och! ye needna fash aboot the loaf for a' the difference a tax on't 'll mak' to you," said Erchie. "If ye gang on the wye ye're daein' wi' the beer, it's the Death Duties yer freends 'll be bothered aboot afore lang." And he led the erring one home.

Big Macphee was the man who for some months back had done the shouting for Duffy's lorry No. 2. He sustained the vibrant penetrating quality of a voice like the Cloch fog-horn on a regimen consisting of beer and the casual hard-boiled egg of the Mull of Kintyre Vaults. He had no relatives except a cousin 'oot aboot Fintry,' and when he justified Erchie's gloomy prediction about the Death Duties by dying of pneumonia a week afterwards, there was none to lament him, save in a mild, philosophical way, except Erchie's wife, Jinnet.

Jinnet, who could never sleep at night till she heard Macphee go up the stairs to his lodgings, thought the funeral would be scandalously cold and heartless lacking the customary "tousy tea" to finish up with, and as Duffy, that particular day, was not in a position to provide this solace for the mourners on their return from Sighthill Cemetery, she invited them to her house. There were Duffy and a man Macphee owed money to; the cousin from 'oot aboot Fintry' and his wife, who was, from the outset, jealous of the genteel way tea was served in Jinnet's parlour, and suspicious of a 'stuckupness' that was only in her own imagination.

"It's been a nesty, wat, mochy, melancholy day far a burial," said

Duffy at the second helping of Jinnet's cold boiled ham; "Macphee was jist as weel oot o't. He aye hated to hae to change his jaicket afore the last rake, him no' haein' ony richt wumman buddy aboot him to dry't."

"Och, the puir cratur!" said Jinnet. "It's like enough he had a disappointment ance upon a time. He was a cheery chap."

"He was a' that," said Duffy. "See's the haud o' the cream-poorie."

The cousin's wife felt Jinnet's home-baked seed-cake was a deliberate taunt at her own inefficiency in the baking line. She sniffed as she nibbled it with a studied appearance of inappreciation. "It wasna a very cheery burial he had, onyway," was her astounding comment, and at that Erchie winked to himself, realising the whole situation.

"Ye're right there, Mistress Grant," said he. "Burials are no' whit they used to be. Perhaps—perhaps ye were expectin' a brass band?" and at that the cousin's wife saw this was a different man from her husband, and that there was a kind of back-chat they have in Glasgow quite unknown in Fintry.

"Oh! I wasna sayin' onything aboot brass bands," she retorted, very red-faced, and looking over to her husband for his support. He, however, was too replete with tea and cold boiled ham for any severe intellectual exercise, and was starting to fill his pipe. "I wasna saying onything aboot brass bands; we're no' used to thae kind o' operatics at burials whaur I come frae. But I think oor ain wye o' funerals is better than the Gleska wye."

Erchie (fearful for a moment that something might have been overlooked) glanced at the fragments of the feast, and at the spirit-bottle that had discreetly circulated somewhat earlier. "We're daein' the best we can," said he. "As shair as death your kizzen—peace be wi' him!—'s jist as nicely buried as if ye paid for it yersel' instead o' Duffy and—and Jinnet; if ye'll no' believe me ye can ask your man. Nae doot Big Macphee deserved as fine a funeral as onybody, wi' a wheen coaches, and a service at the kirk, wi' the organ playin' and a' that, but that wasna the kind o' man your kizzen was when he was livin'. He hated a' kinds o' falderals."

"He was a cheery chap," said Jinnet again, nervously, perceiving some electricity in the air.

"And he micht hae had a nicer burial," said the cousin's wife, with firmness.

"Preserve us!" cried Erchie. "Whit wad ye like?—Flags maybe? Or champagne wine at the liftin'? Or maybe wreaths o' floo'ers? If it was cheeriness ye were wantin' wi' puir Macphee, ye should hae come a month ago and he micht hae ta'en ye himsel' to the Britannia Music-ha'."

"Haud yer tongue, Erchie," said Jinnet; and the cousin's wife, as fast as she could, took all the hair-pins out of her head and put them in again. "They think we're that faur back in Fintry," she said with fine irrelevance.

"Not at all," said Erchie, who saw his innocent wife was getting all the cousin's wife's fierce glances. "Not at all, mem. There's naething wrang wi' Fintry; mony a yin I've sent there. I'm rale chawed we didna hae a Fintry kind o' funeral, to please ye. Whit's the patent thing aboot a Fintry funeral?"

"For wan thing," said the cousin's wife, "it's aye a rale hearse we hae at Fintry and no' a box under a machine, like thon. It was jist a disgrace. Little did his mither think it wad come to thon. Ye wad think it was coals."

"And whit's the maitter wi' coals?" cried Duffy, his professional pride aroused. "Coals was his tred. Ye're shairly awfu' toffs in Fintry aboot yer funerals."

The cousin's wife stabbed her head all over again with her hair-pins, and paid no heed to him. Her husband evaded her eyes with great determination. "No' that great toffs either," she retorted, "but we can aye afford a bit crape. There wasna a sowl that left this close behind the corp the day had crape in his hat except my ain man."

Then the man to whom big Macphee owed money laughed.

"Crape's oot o' date, mistress," Erchie assured her. "It's no' the go noo at a' in Gleska; ye micht as weel expect to see the auld saulies."

"Weel, it's the go enough in Fintry," said the cousin's wife. "And there was anither thing; I didna expect to see onybody else but my man in weepers, him bein' the only freen' puir Macphee had but——"

"I havena seen weepers worn since the year o' the Tay Bridge," said Erchie, "and that was oot at the Mearns."

"Weel, we aye hae them at Fintry," insisted the cousin's wife.

"A cheery chap," said Jinnet again, at her wits'-end to put an end to this restrained wrangling, and the man Big Macphee owed money to laughed again.

"Whit's mair," went on the cousin's wife," my man was the only

15

wan there wi' a decent shirt wi' tucks on the breist o't; the rest o' ye had that sma' respect for the deid ye went wi' shirt-breists as flet as a sheet o' paper. It was showin' awfu' sma' respect for puir Macphee," and she broke down with her handkerchief at her eyes.

"Och! to bleezes! Jessie, ye're spilin' a' the fun," her husband remonstrated.

Erchie pushed back his chair and made an explanation. "Tucks is no' the go naither, mistress," said he, "and if ye kent whit the laundries were in Gleska ye wadna wonder at it. A laundry's a place whaur they'll no stand ony o' yer tucks, or ony nonsense o' that kind. Tucks wad spoil the teeth o' the curry-combs they use in the laundry for scoorin' the cuffs and collars; they're no' gaun awa' to waste the vitriol they use for bleachin' on a wheen tucks. They couldna dae't at the money; it's only threepence ha'penny a shirt, ye ken, and oot o' that they hae to pay for the machines that tak's the button's aff, and the button-hole burster—that's a tred by itsel'. No, mem, tucked breists are oot o' date; ye'll no' see such a thing in Gleska; I'm shair puir Macphee himself hadna ane. The man's as weel buried as if we had a' put on the kilts, and had a piper in front playin' 'Lochaber no More.' If ye'll no believe us, Duffy can show ye the receipted accoonts for the undertaker and the lair; can ye no', Duffy?"

"Smert!" said Duffy.

But the cousin's wife was not at all anxious to see accounts of any kind, so she became more prostrate with annoyance and grief than ever.

"Oot Fintry way," said Erchie, exasperated," it's a' richt to keep up tucked shirt-breists, and crape, and weepers, and mort-cloths, and the like, for there canna be an awfu' lot o' gaiety in the place, but we have aye plenty o' ither things to amuse us in Gleska. There's the Kelvingrove Museum, and the Waxworks. If ye're no' pleased wi' the wye Macphee was buried, ye needna gie us the chance again wi' ony o' yer freen's."

The cousin's wife addressed herself to her husband. "Whit was yon ye were gaun to ask?" she said to him.

He got very red, and shifted uneasily in his chair. "Me!" said he. "I forget."

"No ye dinna; ye mind fine."

"Och, it's a' richt. Are we no' haein' a fine time?" protested the husband.

"No, nor a' richt, Rubbert Grant." She turned to the others. "Whit my man was gaun to ask, if he wasna such a sumph, was whether oor kizzen hadna ony money put by him."

"If ye kent him better, ye wadna need to ask," said Duffy.

"He was a cheery chap," said Jinnet.

"But was he no' in the Shepherds, or the Oddfellows, or the Masons, or onything that wye?"

"No, nor in the Good Templars nor the Rechabites," said Erchie. "The only thing the puir sowl was ever in was the Mull o' Kintyre Vaults."

"Did I no' tell ye?" said her husband.

. . . .

"Good-bye and thenky the noo," said the cousin's wife, as she went down the stair. "I've spent a rale nice day."

"It's the only thing ye did spend," said Erchie when she was out of hearing. "Funerals are managed gey chape in Fintry."

"Oh ye rascal, ye've the sherp tongue!" said Jinnet.

"Ay, and there's some needs it! A flet fit, too, but a warm hert," said Erchie.

17

V

THE PRODIGAL SON

Jinnet, like a wise housewife, aye shops early on Saturday, but she always leaves some errand—some trifle overlooked, as it were—till the evening, for true daughter of the city, she loves at times the evening throng of the streets. That of itself, perhaps, would not send her out with her door-key in her hand and a peering, eager look like that of one expecting something long of coming: the truth is she cherishes a hope that some Saturday to Erchie and her will come what comes often to her in her dreams, sometimes with terror and tears, sometimes with delight.

"I declare, Erchie, if I havena forgotten some sweeties for the kirk the morn," she says; "put on yer kep and come awa' oot wi' me; ye'll be nane the waur o' a breath o' fresh air."

Erchie puts down his 'Weekly Mail,' stifling a sigh and pocketing his spectacles. The night may be raw and wet, the street full of mire, the kitchen more snug and clean and warm than a palace, but he never on such occasion says her nay. "You and your sweeties!" he exclaims, lacing his boots; "I'm shair ye never eat ony, in the kirk or onywhere else."

"And whit dae ye think I wad be buyin' them for if it wasna to keep me frae gantin' in the kirk when the sermon's dreich?"

"Maybe for pappin' at the cats in the back coort," he retorts. "There's ae thing certain shair, I never see ye eatin' them."

"Indeed, and ye're richt," she confesses. "I havena the teeth for them nooadays."

There's naething wrang wi' yer teeth, nor onything else aboot ye that I can see," her husband replies.

"Ye auld haver!" Jinnet will then cry, smiling. "It's you that's lost yer sicht, I'm thinkin'. I'm a done auld buddy, that's whit I am, and that's tellin' ye. But haste ye and come awa' for the sweeties wi' me: whit'll thae wee Wilson weans in the close say the morn if Mrs MacPherson hasna ony sweeties for them?"

They went along New City Road together, Erchie tall, lean, and a little round at the shoulders; his wife a little wee body, not reaching his shoulder, dressed by-ordinar for her station and 'ower young for her years,' as a few jealous neighbours say.

An unceasing drizzle blurred the street lamps, the pavement was slippery with mud; a night for the hearth-side and slippered feet on the fender. Yet, the shops were thronged, and men and women crowded the thoroughfare or stood entranced before the windows.

"It's a wonderfu' place, Gleska," said Erchie. "There's such diversion in't if ye're in the key for't. If ye hae yer health and yer wark, and the weans is weel, ye can be as happy as a lord, and far happier. It's the folk that live in the terraces where the nae stairs is, and sittin' in their paurlours readin' as hard's onything to keep up wi' the times, and naething to see oot the window but a plot o' grass that's no' richt green, that gets tired o' everything. The like o' us, that stay up closes and hae nae servants, and can come oot for a daunder efter turnin' the key in the door, hae the best o't. Lord! there's sae muckle to see—the cheeny-shops and the drapers, and the neighbours gaun for paraffin oil wi' a bottle, and Duffy wi' a new shepherd-tartan grauvit, and Lord Macdonald singin' awa' like a' that at the Normal School, and——"

"Oh, Erchie! dae ye mind when Willie was at the Normal?" said Jinnet.

"Oh, my! here it is already," thought Erchie. "If that laddie o' oors kent the hertbrek he was to his mither, I wonder wad he bide sae lang awa'."

"Yes, I mind, Jinnet; I mind fine. Whit for need ye be askin'? As I was sayin', it's aye in the common streets that things is happenin' that's worth lookin' at, if ye're game for fun. It's like travellin' on the railway; if ye gang first-class, the way I did yince to Yoker by mistake, ye micht as weel be in a herse for a' ye see or hear; but gang third and ye'll aye find something to keep ye cheery if it's only fifteen chaps standin' on yer corns gaun to a fitba'-match, or a man in the corner o' the cairriage wi' a mooth-harmonium playin' a' the wye."

"Oh! Erchie, look at the puir wean," said Jinnet, turning to glance after a woman with an infant in her arms. "Whit a shame bringin' oot weans on a nicht like this! Its face is blae wi' the cauld."

"Och! never mind the weans," said her husband; "if ye were to mind a' the weans ye see in Gleska, ye wad hae a bonnie jot o't."

"But jist think on the puir wee smout, Erchie. Oh, dear me! there's anither yin no' three months auld, I'll wager. It's a black burnin' shame. It should be hame snug and soond in its wee bed. Does't no' mind ye o' Willy when I took him first to his grannie's?"

Her husband growled to himself, and hurried his step, but that night there seemed to be a procession of women with infants in arms in New City Road, and Jinnet's heart was wrung at every crossing. "I thocht it was pan-drops ye cam' oot for, or conversation-losengers," he protested at last; "and here ye're greetin' even-on aboot a wheen weans that's no' oor fault."

"Ye're a hard-herted monster, so ye are," said his wife indignantly.

"Of course I am," he confessed blythely. "I'll throw aff a' disguise and admit my rale name's Bluebeard but don't tell the polis on me. Hard-herted monster—I wad need to be wi' a wife like you, that canna see a wean oot in the street at nicht withoot the drap at yer e'e. The weans is maybee no' that bad aff: the nicht air's no' waur nor the day air: maybe when they're oot here they'll no' mind they're hungry."

"Oh, Erchie! see that puir wee lame yin! God peety him!—I maun gie him a penny," whispered Jinnet, as a child in rags stopped before a jeweller's window to look in on a magic world of silver cruet-stands and diamond rings and gold watches.

"Ye'll dae naething o' the kind!" said Erchie. "It wad jist be wastin' yer money." He pushed his wife on her way past the boy, and, unobserved by her, slipped twopence in the latter's hand.

"I've seen the day ye werena sae mean, Erchie MacPherson," said his wife vexatiously. "Ye aye brag o' yer flet fit and yer warm hert."

"It's jist a sayin'. I'm as mooly's onything," said Erchie, and winked to himself.

It was not the children of the city alone that engaged Jinnet's attention. They came to a street where now and then a young man would come from a public-house staggering; she always scanned the young fool's face with something of expectancy and fear.

"Jist aboot his age, Erchie," she whispered. "Oh, dear! I wonder if that puir callan' has a mither," she stopped to look after the young man in his cups.

Erchie looked too, a little wistfully. "I'll wager ye he has," said he. "And like enough a guid yin, that's no' forgettin' him, though he may gang on the ran-dan, but in her bed at nicht no' sleepin', wonderin' whit's come o' him, and never mindin' onything that was bad in him, but jist a kind o' bein' easy-led, but mindin' hoo smert he was when he was but a laddie, and hoo he won the prize for composeetion in the school, and hoo prood he was when be brocht hame the first wage he got on a Setturday. If God Almichty has the same kind o' memory as a mither, Jinnet, there'll be a chance at the hinderend for the warst o' us."

They had gone at least a mile from home. The night grew wetter and more bitter, the crowds more squalid, Jinnet's interest in errant belated youth more keen. And never a word of the sweets she had made-believe to come out particularly for. They had reached the harbour side. The ships lay black and vacant along the wharfs, noisy seamen and women debauched passed in groups or turned into the public-houses. Far west into the drizzling night the river lamps stretched, showing the drumly water of the highway of the world. Jinnet stopped and looked and listened. "I think we're far enough, Erchie. I think we'll jist gang hame," said she.

"Right! said Erchie, patiently; and they turned, but not without one sad glance from his wife before they lost sight of the black ships, the noisy wharves, the rolling seamen on the pavement, the lamplights of the watery way that reaches to the world's end.

"Oh! Erchie," she said piteously, "I wonder if he's still on the ships."

"Like enough," said her husband. "I'm shair he's no' in Gleska at onyrate without comin' to see us. I'll bate ye he's a mate or a captain or a purser or something, and that thrang somewhere abroad he hasna time the noo; but we'll hear frae him by-and-bye. The wee deevil! I'll gie him't when I see him, to be givin' us such a fricht."

"No' that wee Erchie," said Jinnet. "He's bigger than yersel'."

"So he is, the rascal! am I no' aye thinkin' o' him jist aboot the age he was when he was at the Sunday school."

"Hoolang is't since we heard o' him, Erchie?"

"Three or four years, or maybee five," said Erchie, quickly. "Man! the wye time slips bye! It doesna look like mair than a twelvemonth."

"It looks to me like twenty year," said Jinnet, "and it's naething less than seven, for it was the year o' Annie's weddin', and her wee Alick's six at Mertinmas. Seeven years! Oh, Erchie, where can he be? Whit can be wrang wi' him? No' to write a scrape o' a pen a' that time! Maybee I'll no' be spared to see him again."

"I'll bate ye whit ye like ye will," said her husband. "And if he doesna bring ye hame a lot o' nice things—shells and parrots, and bottles of scent, and Riga Balsam for hacked hands, and the rale Cheena cheeny, and ostrich feathers and a' that, I'll—I'll be awfu' wild at him. But the first thing I'll dae'll be to stand behind the door and catch him when he comes in, and tak' the strap to him for the rideeculous wye he didna write to us."

"Seeven years," said Jinnet. "Oh, that weary sea, a puir trade to be followin' for ony mither's son. It was Australia he wrote frae last; whiles I'm feared they catched him oot there and killed him in the Bush."

"No! nor the Bush! Jist let them try it wi' oor Willie! Dod! he would put the hems on them; he could wrastle a score o' those fellows wi' his least wee bit touch."

"Erchie."

"Weel, Jinnet?"

"Ye'll no' be angry wi' me; but wha was it tellt ye they saw him twa years syne carryin' on near the quay, and that he was stayin' at the Sailors' Home?"

"It was Duffy," said Erchie, hurriedly. "I have a guid mind to—to kick him for sayin' onything o' the kind. I wad hae kicked him for't afore this if—if I wasna a beadle in the kirk."

"I'm shair it wasna oor Willie at a'," said Jinnet.

"Oor Willie! Dae ye think the laddie's daft, to be in Gleska and no' come to see his mither?"

"I canna believe he wad dae't," said Jinnet, but always looked intently in the face of every young man who passed them.

.   .   .   .

"Weel, that's ower for anither Setturday," said Erchie to himself, resuming his slippers and his spectacles.

"I declare, wife," said he, "ye've forgotten something."

"Whit is't?" she asked.

"The sweeties ye went oot for," said Erchie, solemnly.

"Oh, dear me! amn't I the silly yin? Thinkin' on that Willie o' oors puts everything oot o' my heid."

Erchie took a paper bag from his pocket and handed it to her. "There ye are," said he. "I had them in my pooch since dinner-time. I kent ye wad be needin' them."

"And ye never let on, but put on your boots and cam' awa' oot wi' me."

"Of coorse I did; I'm shairly no' that auld but I can be gled on an excuse for a walk oot wi' my lass?"

"Oh, Erchie! Erchie!" she cried, "when will ye be wise? I think I'll put on the kettle and mak' a cup o' tea to ye."

VI

MRS DUFFY DESERTS HER MAN

"They're yatterin' awa' in the papers there like sweetie-wives aboot Carlyle and his wife," said Erchie. "It's no' the thing at a' makin' an exposure. I kent Carlyle fine; he had a wee baker's shop in Balmano Brae, and his wife made potted heid. It was quite clean; there was naething wrang wi't. If they quarrelled it was naebody's business but their ain.

"It's a gey droll hoose whaur there's no' whiles a rippit. Though my fit's flet my hert's warm; but even me and Jinnet hae a cast-oot noo and then. I'm aye the mair angry if I ken I'm wrang, and I've seen me that bleezin' bad-tempered that I couldna light my pipe, and we wadna speak to ane anither for oors and oors.

"It'll come the nicht, and me wi' a job at waitin' to gang to, and my collar that hard to button I nearly break my thumbs.

"For a while Jinnet'll say naethin', and then she'll cry, 'See's a haud o't, ye auld fuiter!'

"I'll be glowerin' awfu' solemn up at the corner o' the ceilin' when she's workin' at the button, lettin' on I'm fair ferocious yet, and she'll say, 'Whit are ye glowerin' at? Dae ye see ony spiders' webs?'

'No, nor spiders' webs,' I says, as gruff as onything. 'I never saw a spider's web in this hoose.'

"At that she gets red in the face and tries no' to laugh."

'There ye are laughin'! Ye're bate!' I says.

'So are you laughin',' says she; 'and I saw ye first. Awa', ye're daft! Will I buy onything tasty for your supper?'

"Duffy's different. I'm no' blamin' him, for his wife's different too. When they quarrel it scandalises the close and gies the land a bad name. The wife washes even-on, and greets into her washin'-byne till she mak's the water cauld, and Duffy sits a' nicht wi' his feet on the kitchen-hobs singin' 'Boyne Water,' because her mither was a Bark, called M'Ginty, and cam' frae Connaught. The folk in the flet above them hae to rap doon at them wi' a poker afore they'll get their nicht's sleep, and the broken delf that gangs oot to the ash-pit in the mornin' wad fill a crate.

"I'm no' sayin', mind ye, that Duffy doesna like her; it's jist his wye, for he hasna ony edication. He was awfu' vexed the time she broke her leg; it pit him aff his wark for three days, and he spent the time lamentin' aboot her doon in the Mull o' Kintyre Vaults.

MY DROLL FRIEND

"The biggest row they ever had that I can mind o' was aboot the time the weemen wore the dolmans. Duffy's wife took the notion o' a dolman, and told him that seein' there was a bawbee up in the bag o' coal that week, she thocht he could very weel afford it.

'There's a lot o' things we'll hae to get afore the dolman,' says he; 'I'm needin' a new kep mysel', and I'm in a menoj for a bicycle.'

'I'm fair affronted wi' my claes,' says she; 'I havena had onything new for a year or twa, and there's Carmichael's wife wi' her sealskin jaicket.'

'Let her!' says Duffy; 'wi' a face like thon she's no' oot the need o't.'

"They started wi' that and kept it up till the neighbours near brocht doon the ceilin' on them."

'That's the worst o' leevin' in a close,' said Duffy, 'ye daurna show ye're the maister in yer ain hoose withoot a lot o' nyafs above ye spilin' a' the plaister.'

"Duffy's wife left him the very next day, and went hame to her mither's. She left oot clean sox for him and a bowl o' mulk on the dresser in case he micht be hungry afore he could mak' his ain tea.

"When Duffy cam' hame and found whit had happened, he was awfu' vexed for himsel' and begood to greet.

"I heard aboot the thing, and went in to see him, and found him drinkin' the mulk and eatin' shaves o' breid at twa bites to the shave the same as if it was for a wager."

'Isn't this an awfu' thing that's come on me. MacPherson?' says he; 'I'm nae better than a weedower except for the mournin's.'

'It hasna pit ye aff yer meat onywye,' says I.

'Oh!' he says, 'ye may think I'm callous, but I hae been greetin' for twa oors afore I could tak' a bite, and I'm gaun to start again as soon as I'm done wi' this mulk.'

'Ye should gang oot,' I tells him, 'and buy the mistress a poke o' grapes and gang roond wi't to her mither's and tell her ye're an eediot and canna help it.'

"But wad he? No fears o' him!"

'Oh! I can dae fine withoot her,' he tells me quite cocky. 'I could keep a hoose wi' my least wee bit touch.'

'Ye puir deluded crature,' I tell't him, 'ye micht as well try to keep a hyena. It looks gey like a collie-dug, but it'll no' sup saps, and a hoose looks an awfu' simple thing till ye try't; I ken fine because Jinnet aften tellt me.'

24

"He begood to soop the floor wi' a whitenin'-brush, and put the stour under the bed."

'Go on,' says I, 'ye're daein' fine for a start. A'ye want's a week or twa at the nicht-schools, where they learn ye laundry-work and cookin', and when ye're at it ye should tak' lessons in scientific dressmakin'. I'll look for ye comin' up the street next week wi' the charts under your oxter and your lad wi' ye.'

"For a hale week Duffy kept his ain hoose.

"He aye forgot to buy sticks for the fire at nicht, and had to make' it in the mornin' wi' a dizzen or twa o' claes-pins. He didna mak' tea, for he couldna tak' tea withoot cream till't, and he couldna get cream because he didna ken the wye to wash a poorie, so he made his breakfast o' cocoa and his tea o' cocoa till he was gaun aboot wi' a broon taste in his mooth.

"On the Sunday he tried to mak' a dinner, and biled the plates wi' soap and soda to get the creesh aff them when he found it wadna come aff wi' cauld water and a washin'-clout."

'Hoo are ye gettin' on in yer ain bonny wee hoose noo?' I asks him ae dirty, wet, cauld day, takin' a bowl o' broth to him frae Jinnet.

'Fine,' says he, quite brazen; 'it's like haein' a yacht. I could be daein' first-rate if it was the summer-time.'

"He wore them long kahootchy boots up to your knees on wet days at his wark, and he couldna get them aff him withoot a hand frae his wife, so he had jist to gang to his bed wi' them on. He ordered pipe-clay by the hunderwicht and soap by the yard; he blackleaded his boots, and didna gang to the kirk because he couldna get on his ain collar.

'Duffy,' I says, 'ye'll make' an awfu' nice and auld wife if ye leeve lang enough. I'll hae to get Jinnet started to knit ye a Shetland shawl.'

"Efter a week it begood to tell awfu' bad on Duffy's health. He got that thin, and so wake in the voice he lost orders, for a wheen o' his auldest customers didna ken him when he cried, and gave a' their tred to MacTurk, the coalman, that had a wife and twa sisters-in-law to coother him up wi' beef-tea on wet days and a' his orders.

"Duffy's mind was affected too; he gave the richt wicht, and lost two chances in ae day o' pittin' a ha'penny on the bag wi' auld blin' weemen that couldna read his board.

"Then he ca'd on a doctor. The doctor tell't him he couldna mak' it oot at a', but thocht it was appen—what d'ye ca't?—the same trouble as the King had, and that Duffy had it in five or six different places. There was naething for him but carefu' dietin' and a voyage to the Cape.

"That very day Duffy, gaun hame frae his wark gey shauchly, wi' a tin o' salmon in his pooch for his tea, saw his wife comin' doon the street. When she saw him she turned and ran awa', and him efter her as hard's he could pelt. She thocht he was that wild he was gaun to gie her a clourin'; and she was jist fair bate wi' the runnin' when he caught up on her in a back coort."

'Tig!' says Duffy, touchin' her; 'you're het!'

'Oh, Jimmy!' she says, 'are ye in wi' me?'

'Am I no'?' says Duffy, and they went hame thegither.

'There was a stranger in my tea this mornin',' says Duffy: 'I kent fine somebody wad be comin'.'

"His wife tell't Jinnet a while efter that that she was a great deal the better o' the rest she got the time she went hame to her mither's; it was jist the very thing she was needin'; and forbye, she got the dolman."

VII

CARNEGIE'S WEE LASSIE

Erchie sought me out on Saturday with a copy of that day's 'News' containing a portrait of Carnegie's little daughter Margaret. "Man, isn't she the rale wee divert?" said he, glowing. "That like her faither, and sae weel-put-on! She minds me terrible o' oor wee Teenie when she was jist her age."

"She has been born into an enviable state, Erchie," I said.

"Oh, I'm no' sae shair aboot that," said Erchie. "It's a gey hard thing, bein' a millionaire's only wean. She canna hae mony wee lassies like hersel' to play the peever wi', or lift things oot o' the stank o' Skibo Castle wi' a bit o' clye and a string. I'm shair it must be a hard job for the auld man, her paw, to provide diversions for the puir wee smout. And she'll hae that mony things that she'll no' can say whit she wants next. I ken fine the wye it'll be up yonder at Skibo.

"It'll be, 'Paw, I'm wantin' something.'

'Whit is't, my dawtie, and ye'll get it to break?' Mr Carnegie 'll say, and lift her on his knee, and let her play wi' the works o' his two thoosand pound repeater watch.

'I dinna ken,' says the wee lassie, 'but I want it awfu' fast.'

'Whit wad ye be sayin' to an electric doll wi' a phonograph inside it to mak' it speak?' asks Mr Carnegie.

'I'm tired o' dolls,' says the wee yin, 'and, besides, I wad raither dae the speakin' mysel'.'

'Ye're a rale wee woman there, Maggie,' says her paw.

'Weel, whit dae ye say to a wee totey motor-car a' for your ain sel', and jewelled in four-and-twenty holes?' says he efter that, takin' the hands o' his watch frae her in case she micht swallow them.

'Oh! a motor-car,' says the wee lassie. 'No, I'm no carin' for ony mair motor-cars; I canna get takin' them to my bed wi' me.'

'Ye're weel aff there,' says he. 'I've had the hale o' the Pittsburg works to my bed wi' me,' he says. 'They were in my heid a' the time when I couldna' sleep, and they were on my chest a' the time when I was sleepin'.'

'Whit wye that, paw?' says the wee lassie.

'I was feart something wad gae wrang, and I wad lose a' the tred, and be puir again.'

'But I thocht ye wanted to die puir, paw?' says the wee lassie.

27

'Ay, but I never had ony notion o' living puir,' says Mr Carnegie as smert's ye like, 'and that mak's a' the difference. If ye're no' for anither motor carriage, wad ye no' tak' a new watch?'

'No, paw,' says the wee lassie, 'I'm no' for anither watch. The only thing a watch tells ye is when it's time to gang to bed, and then I'm no wantin' to gang onywye. Whit I wad like wad be ane o' thae watches that had haunds that dinna move when ye're haein' awfu' fine fun.'

'Oh, ay!' says her paw at that; 'that's the kind we're a' wantin', but they're no' makin' them, and I'm no' shair that I wad hae muckle use for yin nooadays even if they were. If ye'll no hae a watch, will ye hae a yacht, or a brass band, or a fleein'-machine, or a piebald pony?'

'I wad raither mak' mud-pies,' says the wee innocent.

'Mud-pies!' cries her faither in horror, lookin' roond to see that naebody heard her. 'Wheesh! Maggie, it wadna look nice to see the like o' you makin' mud-pies. Ye havena the claes for't. Beside, I'm tellt they're no' the go nooadays at a'.'

'Weel,' says she at that, 'I think I'll hae a hairy-heided lion.'

'Hairy-heided lion. Right!' says Mr Carnegie. 'Ye'll get that, my wee lassie,' and cries doon the turret stair to the kitchen for his No.9 secretary.

"The No.9 secretary comes up in his shirt sleeves, chewin' blot-sheet and dichting the ink aff his elbows.

'Whit are ye thrang at the noo?' asks Mr Carnegie as nice as onything to him, though he's only a kind o' a workin' man.

'Sendin' aff the week's orders for new kirk organs,' says the No.9 secretary, 'and it'll tak' us till Wednesday.'

'Where's a' the rest o' my secretaries?' asks Mr Carnegie.

'Half o' them's makin' oot cheques for new leebraries up and doon the country, and the ither half's oot in the back-coort burning letters frae weedows wi' nineteen weans, nane o' them daein' for themsel's, and frae men that were dacent and steady a' their days, but had awfu' bad luck.'

'If it gangs on like this we'll hae to put ye on the night-shift,' says Mr Carnegie. 'It's comin' to't when I hae to write ma ain letters. I'll be expected to write my ain books next. But I'll no' dae anything o' the kind. Jist you telegraph to India, or Africa, or Japan, or wherever the hairy-heided lions comes frae, and tell them to sent wee Maggie ane o' the very best at 50 per cent. aff for cash.'

"Early ae mornin' some weeks efter that, when the steam-hooter for wakenin' the secretaries starts howlin' at five o'clock, Mr Carnegie comes doon stair and sees the hairy-heided lion in a crate bein' pit aff a lorry. He has it wheeled in to the wee lassie when she's at her breakfast.

'Let it oot,' she says; 'I want to play wi't.'

'Ye wee fuiter!' he says laughin' like onything, 'ye canna get playin' wi't oot o' the cage, but ye'll can get feedin't wi' sultana-cake.'

"But that disna suit wee Maggie, and she jist tells him to send it awa' to the Bronx Zoo in New York."

'Bronx Zoo. Right!' says her paw, and cries on his No.22 secretary to send it aff wi' the parcel post at yince.

'That minds me,' he says, 'there's a cryin' need for hairy-heided lions all over Europe and the United States. The moral and educative influence o' the common or bald-heided lion is no account. Noo that maist o' the kirks has twa organs apiece, and there's a leebrary in every clachan in the country, I must think o' some ither wye o' gettin' rid o' this cursed wealth. It was rale 'cute o' you Maggie, to think o't; I'll pay half the price o' a hairy-heided lion for every toon in the country wi' a population o' over five hundred that can mak' up the ither half by public subscription.'

"And then the wee lassie says she canna tak' her parridge."

'Whit for no'? he asks her, anxious-like. 'Are they no guid?'

'Oh, they're maybe guid enough,' she says, 'but I wad raither hae toffie.'

'Toffie. Right!' says her paw, and orders up the chef to mak' toffie in a hurry.

'Whit's he gaun to mak' it wi'?' asks the wee yin.

'Oh, jist in the ordinar' wye—wi' butter and sugar,' says her paw.

'That's jist common toffie,' says the wee lassie; 'I want some ither kind.'

'As shair's death, Maggie,' he says, 'there's only the ae wye o' makin' toffie'

'Then whit's the use o' haein' a millionaire for a paw?' she asks.

'True for you,' he says, and thinks hard. 'I could mak' the chef put in champed rubies or a di'mond or twa grated doon.'

'Wad it mak' the toffie taste ony better?' asks the wee cratur'.

'No' a bit better,' he says. 'It wadna taste sae guid as the ordinary toffie, but it wad be nice and dear.'

'Then I'll jist hae to hae the plain, chape toffie,' says wee Maggie. 'That's jist whit I hae to hae mysel' wi' a great mony things,' says her paw. 'Being a millionaire's nice enough some wyes, but there's a wheen things money canna buy, and paupers wi' three or four thoosand paltry pounds a-year is able to get jist as guid toffie and ither things as I can. I canna even dress mysel' different frae ither folks, for it was look rideeculous to see me gaun aboot wi' gold cloth waistcoats and a hat wi' strings o' pearls on it, so' a' I can dae is to get my nickerbocker suits made wi' an extra big check. I hae the pattern that big noo there's only a check-and-a-half to the suit; but if it wasna for the honour o't I wad just as soon be wearin' Harris tweed.'

"Upon my word, Erchie," I said, "you make me sorry for our philanthropic friend, and particularly for his little girl."

"Oh, there's no occasion!" protested Erchie. "There's no condeetion in life that hasna its compensations, and even Mr Carnegie's wee lassie has them. I hae nae doot the best fun her and her paw gets is when they're playin' at bein' puir. The auld man 'll nae doot whiles hides his pocket-money in the press, and sit doon readin' his newspaper, wi' his feet on the chimney-piece, and she'll come in and ask for a bawbee.

'I declare to ye I havena a farden, Maggie,' he'll say; 'but I'll gie ye a penny on Setturday when I get my pay.'

'I dinna believe ye,' she'll say.

'Then ye can ripe me,' says her paw, and the wee tot'll feel in a' his pooches, and find half a sovereign in his waistcoat. They'll let on it's jist a bawbee (the wee thing never saw a rale bawbee in her life, I'll warrant), and he'll wonner whit wye he forgot aboot it, and tell her to keep it and buy jujubes wi't, and she'll be awa' like a whitteruck and come back in a while wi' her face a' sticky for a kiss, jist like rale.

"Fine I ken the wee smouts; it was that wye wi' oor ain Teenie.

"Other whiles she'll hae a wee tin bank wi' a bee-skep on't, and she'll hae't fu' o' sovereigns her faither's veesitors slip't in her haund when they were gaun awa', and she'll put it on the mantelpiece and gang out. Then her paw'll get up laughin' like onything to himsel', and tak' doon the wee bank and rattle awa' at it, lettin' on he's robbin't for a schooner o' beer, and at that she'll come rinnin' in a catch him at it, and they'll hae great fun wi' that game. I have nae doot her faither and mither get mony a laugh at her playin' at wee washin's, too, and lettin' on she's fair trauchled aff the face o' the earth wi' a family o' nine dolls, an' three o' them doon wi' the hoopin'-cough. Oh! they're no that bad aff for fine fun even in Skibo Castle."

VIII
A SON OF THE CITY

My old friend came daundering down the street with what might have been a bag of cherries, if cherries were in season, and what I surmised were really the twopenny pies with which Jinnet and he sometimes made the Saturday evenings festive. When we met he displayed a blue hyacinth in a flower-pot.

"Saw't in a fruiterer's window," said he, "and took the notion. Ninepence; dod! I dinna ken hoo they mak' them for the money. I thocht it wad please the wife, and min' her o' Dunoon and the Lairgs and a' thae places that's doon the watter in the summer-time.

"Ye may say whit ye like, I'm shair they shut up a' thae coast toons when us bonny wee Gleska buddies is no' comin' doon wi' oor tin boxes, and cheerin' them up wi' a clog-wallop on the quay.

"It's a fine thing a flooer; no' dear to buy at the start, and chaper to keep than a canary. It's Nature—the Rale Oreeginal. Ninepence! And the smell o't! Jist a fair phenomena!"

"A sign of spring, Erchie," I said; "thank heaven! the primrose is in the wood, and the buds bursting on the hedge in the country, though you and I are not there to see it."

"I daursay," said he, "I'll hae to mak' a perusal doon the length o' Yoker on the skoosh car when the floods is ower. I'm that used to them noo, as shair's death I canna get my naitural sleep on dry nichts unless Jinnet gangs oot to the back and throws chuckies at the window, lettin' on it's rain and hailstanes. When I hear the gravel on the window I cod mysel' it's the genuine auld Caledonian climate, say my wee 'Noo I lay me,' and gang to sleep as balmy as a nicht polisman.

"There's a great cry the noo aboot folks comin' frae the country and croodin' into the toons and livin' in slums and degenerating the bone and muscle o' Britain wi' eatin' kippered herrin' and ice-cream. Thoosands o' them's gaun aboot Gleska daein' their bit turns the best way they can, and no' kennin', puir craturs, there's a Commission sittin' on them as hard's it can."

'Whit's wanted,' says the Inspectors o' Poor, 'is to hustle them aboot frae place to place till the soles o' their feet gets red-hot wi' the speed they're gaun at; then gie them a bar o' carbolic soap and a keg o' Keatin' poother, and put them on the first train for Edinburgh.'

'Tear doon the rookeries,' says anither man, 'and pit up rooms and kitchens wi' wally jawboxes and tiled closes at a rent o' eighteenpence a-week when ye get it.'

'That's a' very fine,' says the economists, 'but if ye let guid wally jawbox hooses at ten shillin's a-year less than the auld-established and justly-pupular slum hoose, will't no' tempt mair puir folk frae the country into Gleska and conjest the Gorbals worse then ever?'

"The puir economists thinks the folks oot aboot Skye and Kamerhashinjoo's waitin' for telegrams tellin' them the single apairment hoose in Lyon Street, Garscube Road, 's doon ten shillin's a-year, afore they pack their carpet-bags and start on the *Clansman* for the Broomielaw. But they're no'. They divna ken onything aboot the rent o' hooses in Gleska, and they're no' carin', for maybe they'll no' pay't onywye. They jist come awa' to Gleska when the wife tells them, and Hughie's auld enough for a polisman.

"Slums! wha wants to abolish slums? It's no' the like o' me nor Duffy. If there werena folk leevin' in slums I couldna buy chape shirts, and the celebrated Stand Fast Craigroyston serge breeks at 2s. 11d. the pair, bespoke, guaranteed, shrunk, and wan hip-pocket.

"When they're proposin' the toast o' the 'Army, Navy, and Reserve Forces,' they ought to add the Force that live in Slums. They're the men and women that's aye ready to sweat for their country—when their money's done. A man that wants the chapest kind o' chape labour kens he'll aye can get it in the slums. If it wasna for that, my Stand Fast Craigroyston breeks wad maybe cost 7s. 6d., and some of the elders in the kirk I'm beadle for wad hae to smoke tuppenny cigars instead o' sixpenny yins.

"The slums 'll no' touch ye if ye don't gang near them.

"Whit a lot o' folk want to dae 's to run the skoosh cars away oot into the country whaur the clegs and the midges and the nae gas is, and coup them oot at Deid Slow on the Clyde, and leave them there wander't. Hoo wad they like it themsel's? The idea is that Duffy, when he's done wi' his last rake o' coals, 'll mak' the breenge for Deid Slow, and tak' his tea and wash his face wi' watter that hard it stots aff his face like a kahootchy ba', and spend a joyous and invigoratin' evenin' sheuchin' leeks and prunin' cauliflooer-bushes in the front plot o' his cottage home.

"I think I see him! He wad faur sooner pay twelve pounds rent in Grove Street, and hae the cheery lowe o' the Mull o' Kintyre Vaults forenent his paurlor window, than get his boots a' glaur wi' plantin' syboes roond his cottage home at £6, 10s.

"The country's a' richt for folks that havena their health and dinna want to wear a collar to their wark, and Deid Slow and places like that may be fine for gaun to if ye want to get ower the dregs o' the measles, but they're nae places for ony man that loves his fellow-men.

"And still there's mony a phenomena! I ken a man that says he wad stay in the country a' the year roond if he hadna to bide in Gleska and keep his eye on ither men in the same tred's himsel', to see they're no' risin' early in the mornin' and gettin' the better o' him.

"It wadna suit Easy-gaun Erchie. Fine I ken whit the country is; did I no' live a hale winter aboot Dalry when I was a halflin'?

"It's maybe a' richt in summer, when you and me gangs oot on an excursion, and cheers them up wi' our melodean wi' bell accompaniment, but the puir sowls havena much diversion at the time o' year the V-shaped depression's cleckin' on Ben Nevis, and the weather prophets in the evening papers is promisin' a welcome change o' weather every Setturday. All ye can dae when your wark's done and ye've ta'en your tea 's to put on a pair o' top-boots and a waterproof, and gang oot in the dark. There's no' even a close to coort in, and if ye want to walk along a country road at nicht thinking' hoo much money ye hae in the bank, ye must be gey smert no' to fa' into a ditch. Stars? Wha wants to bother glowerin' at stars? There's never ony change in the programme wi' them in the country. If I want stars I gang to the Britannia.

"Na, na, Gleska's the place, and it's nae wonder a' the country-folks is croodin' into't as fast's they can get their cottage homes sublet.

"This is the place for intellect and the big pennyworth of skim-milk.

"I declare I'm that ta'en wi' Gleska I get up sometime afore the fire's lichted to look oot at the window and see if it's still to the fore.

"Fifteen public-hooses within forty yairds o' the close-mooth, a guttapercha works at the tap o' the street, and twa cab-stances at the foot. My mornin' 'oors are made merry wi' the delightfu' strains o' factory hooters and the sound o' the dust-cart man kickin' his horse like onything whaur it'll dae maist guid.

"I can get onywhere I want to gang on the skoosh cars for a bawbee or a penny, but the only place I hae to gang to generally is my wark, and I wad jist as soon walk it for I'm no' in ony hurry.

"When the rain's blashin' doon at nicht on the puir miserable craturs workin' at their front plots in Deid Slow, or trippin' ower hens that'll no' lay ony eggs, I can be improvin' my mind wi' Duffy at the Mull o' Kintyre Vaults, or daunderin' alang the Coocaddens wi' my hand tight on my watchpocket, lookin' at the shop windows and jinkin' the members o' the Sons of Toil Social Club (Limited), as they tak' the breadth o' the pavement.

"Gleska! Some day when I'm in the key for't I'll mak' a song aboot her. Here the triumphs o' civilisation meet ye at the stair-fit, and three bawbee mornin' rolls can be had efter six o'clock at nicht for a penny.

"There's libraries scattered a' ower the place, I ken, for I've seen them often, and the brass plate at the door tellin' ye whit they are.

"Art's a' the go in Gleska, too. There's something aboot it every ither nicht in the papers, when Lord Somebody-or-ither's no' divorcin' his wife, and takin' up the space. And I hear there's hunders o' pictures oot in yon place at Kelvingrove.

"Theatres, concerts, balls, swarees, lectures—ony mortal thing ye like that'll keep ye oot o' your bed, ye'll get in Gleska if ye have the money to pay for't."

"It's true, Erchie."

"Whit's true?" said the old man, wrapping the paper more carefully round his flower-pot. "Man, I'm only coddin'. Toon or country, it doesna muckle maitter if like me, ye stay in yer ain hoose. I don't stay in Gleska; not me! it's only the place I mak' my money in; I stay wi' Jinnet."

IX

ERCHIE ON THE KING'S CRUISE

I deliberately sought out Erchie one day in order to elicit his views upon the Royal progress through the Western Isles, and found him full of the subject, with the happiest disposition to eloquence thereon.

"Man! I'm that gled I'm to the fore to see this prood day for Scotland," said he. "I'm daein' hardly onything but read the mornin' and evenin' papers, and if the Royal yacht comes up the length o' Yoker I'm gaun doon mysel' to wave a hanky. 'His Majesty in Arran. Great Reception,' says they. 'His Majesty in Glorious Health. Waves his hand to a Wee Lassie, and Nearly Shoots a Deer,' says they. 'His Majesty's Yacht Surrounded by the Natives. Escape round the Mull. Vexation of Campbeltown, and Vote of Censure by the Golfers of Machrihanish,' says they. Then the telegrams frae 'Oor Special Correspondent': 'Oban, 1 P.M.—It is confidently expected that the Royal yacht will come into the bay this evenin' in time for tea. The esplanade is being washed with eau-de-Cologne, and a' the magistrates is up at Rankine's barbar shop gettin' a dry shampoo.' 'Oban, 1.30 P.M.—A wire frae Colonsay says the Royal yacht is about to set sail for Oban. Tremendous excitement prevails here, and the price o' hotel bedrooms is raised 200 per cent. It is decided to mobilise the local Boys' Brigade, and engage Johnny McColl to play the pipes afore the King when he's comin' ashore.' '6 P.M.—The Royal yacht has just passed Kerrara, and it is now certain that Oban will not be visited by the Royal party. All the flags have been taken down, and scathing comments on the extraordinary affair are anticipated from the local Press.'

"Maybe ye wadna think it, but his Majesty's gaun roond the West Coast for the sake o' his health."

'Ye'll hae to tak' a month o' the rest cure,' the doctors tellt him, 'a drap o' claret wine to dinner, and nae worry aboot business.'

'Can I afford it?' said his Majesty, that vexed-like, for he was puttin' aff his coat and rollin' up his sleeves to start work for the day.

'There's nae choice in the maitter,' said the doctors, 'we order it.'

'But can I afford it?' again said his Majesty. 'Ye ken yoursel's, doctors, I have had a lot o' expense lately, wi' trouble in the hoose, and wi' the Coronation and aething and another. Could I no' be doin' the noo wi' Setturday-to-Monday trips doon the watter?'

"But no; the doctors said there was naethin' for him but rest. So his Majesty had to buy a new topcoat and a yachtin' bunnet, and start oot on the *Victoria and Albert*.

"It's a twa-funnelled boat, but I'm tellt that, bein' Government built, yin o' the funnels has a blaw-doon, and they daurna light the furnace below't if the win's no' in a certain airt.

"The yacht made first for the Isle o' Man, and wasna five meenutes in the place when the great novelist, Hall Corelli or Mary Caine, or whichever it is, was aboard o' her distributin' hand-bills advertisin' the latest novel, and the King took fright, and left the place as soon as he could.

"I'm tellin' ye it's a gey sair trauchle bein' a King. The puir sowl thought the Hielan's wad be a nice quate place where naebody wad bother him, and so he set sail then for Arran."

'What is that I see afore me?' said he, comin' up past Pladda.

"The captain put his spy-gless to his e'e, and got as white's a cloot.

'It's your Majesty's joyous and expectant subjects,' says he. 'They've sixty-seven Gleska steamers oot yonder waitin' on us, and every skipper has his hand on the string o' the steam-hooter.'

'My God!' groaned the puir King, 'I thought I was sent awa' here for the guid o' my health.'

"Before he could say knife, a' the Gleska steamers and ten thoosan' wee rowin'-boats were scrapin' the pent aff the sides o' the *Victoria and Albert*, and half a million Scottish taxpayers were cheerin' their beloved Sovereign, Edward VII., every mortal yin o' them sayin', "Yon's him yonder!' and p'intin' at him.

'Will I hae to shoogle hands wi' a' that crood?' he asked the captain o' the *Victoria and Albert*, and was told it wad dae if he jist took aff his kep noo and then.

"And so, takin' aff his kep noo and then, wi' a' the Gleska steamers and the ten thoosan' wee rowin'-boats hingin' on to the side o' the yacht, and half a million devoted subjects takin' turn aboot at keekin' in through the port-holes to see what he had for dinner, his Majesty sailed into Brodick Bay.

'The doctors were right,' says he; 'efter a', there's naething like a rest cure; it's a mercy we're a' spared.'

"The following day his Majesty hunted the deer in Arran. I see frae the papers that he was intelligently and actively assisted in this by the well-known ghillies, Dugald McFadyen, Donald Campbell, Sandy McNeill, and Peter McPhedran.

"They went up the hill and picked oot a nice quate he-deer, and drove it doon in front o' where his Majesty sat beside a stack o' loaded guns. His Majesty was graciously pleased to tak' up yin o' the guns, and let bang at the deer.

'Weel done! That wass gey near him,' said Dugald McFadyen, strikin' the deer wi' his stick to mak' it stop eatin' the gress.

"His Majesty fired a second time, and the deer couldna stand it ony langer, but went aff wi' a breenge.

'Weel, it's a fine day to be oot on the hull onywye,' says McPhedran, resigned-like, and the things that the heid ghillie Campbell didna say was terrible.

"The papers a' said the deer was shot, and a bloody business too; but it wasna till lang efter the cauld-clye corpse o't was found on the hill."

'Here it is!' said McFadyen.

'I daursay it is,' said McNeill.

'It'll hae to be it onywye,' said the heid man, and they had it weighed.

"If it was sold in Gleska the day it would fetch ten shillin's a-pound.

"If there's ae thing I've noticed mair than anither aboot Heilan' ghillies, it's that they'll no hurt your feelin's if they can help it. I'm Hielan' mysel'; my name's MacPherson; a flet fit but a warm hert, and I ken.

"Meanwhile Campbeltoon washed its face, put a clove in its mooth, and tried to look as spruce as it could for a place that has mair distilleries than kirks. The Royal veesit was generally regairded as providential, because the supremacy o' Speyside whiskies over Campbeltoon whiskies o' recent years wad hae a chance o' being overcome if his Majesty could be prevailed on to gang through a' the distilleries and hae a sample frae each o' them.

"It was to be a gala day, and the bellman went roond the toon orderin' every loyal ceetizen to put oot a flag, cheer like onything when the King was gaun to the distilleries, and bide inside their hooses when he was comin' back frae them. But ye'll no' believ't— THE YACHT PASSED CAMPBELTOON!

"The Provost and Magistrates and the hale community was doon on the quay to cairry the Royal pairty shouther high if necessary, and when they saw the *Victoria and Albert* they cheered sae lood they could be heard the length o' Larne.

'Whit's that?' said his Majesty.

'By the smell o't I wad say Campbeltoon,' said his skipper, 'and that's mair o' your Majesty's subjects, awfu' interested in your recovery.'

'Oh man!' said the puir King, nearly greetin', 'we divna ken whit health is, ony o' us, till we lose it. Steam as far aff frae the shore as ye can, and it'll maybe no' be sae bad.'

"So the yacht ran bye Campbeltoon. The folk couldna believe't at first."

'They must hae made a mistake,' says they; 'perhaps they didna notice the distillery lums,' and the polis sergeant birled his whustle by order of the Provost, to ca' the King's attention, but it was to no avail, a rale divert!

"The yacht went on to Colonsay.

"That's the droll thing aboot this trip o' his Majesty's; it's no' ony nice, cheery sort o' places he gangs to at a', but oot-o'-the-wye wee places wi' naethin' aboot them but hills and things—wee trashy places wi' nae braw new villas aboot them, and nae minstrels or banjo-singers, on the esplanade singin' 'O! Lucky Jim!' and clautin' in the bawbees. I divna suppose they had half a dizzen flags in a' Colonsay, and ye wad fancy the King's een's no' that sair lookin' at flags but whit he wad be pleased to see mair o' them.

"Colonsay! Man, it's fair peetifu'! No' a Provost or a Bylie in't to hear a bit speech frae; nae steamboat trips to gang roond the Royal yacht and keek in the portholes; but everything as quate as a kirk on a Setturday mornin'.

"A' the rest o' Scotland wanted to wag flags at his Majesty Edward VII., and here he maun put up at Colonsay! The thing was awfu' badly managed.

"If Campbeltoon was chawed at the yacht passin' withoot giein' a cry in, whit's to describe the vexation o' Oban?

"Oban had its hert set on't. It never occured to the mind o' Oban for wan meeute that the King could pass the 'Chairin' Cross o' the Hielan's' withoot spendin' a week there at the very least, and everything was arranged to mak' the Royal convalescent comfortable.

"The bay was fair jammed wi' yachts, and a' the steam-whustles were oiled. The hotels were packed to the roof wi' English tourists, some o' them sleepin' under the slates, wi' their feet in the cisterns, and gled to pay gey dear for the preevilege o' breathin' the same air as Edward VII.

"Early in the day somebody sent the alarmin' tidin's frae Colonsay that the *Victoria and Albert* micht pass Oban efter a', and to prevent this, herrin'-nets were stretched aff Kerrara to catch her if ony such dastardly move was made.

"But is was nae use; Oban's in sackcloth and ashes.

'Where are we noo?' asked the Royal voyager, aff Kerrara. 'Is this Shingleton-on-the-Sea?'

'No, your Majesty,' says the skipper of the Royal yacht, 'it's Oban, the place whaur the German waiters get their education.'

'Heavens!' cried his Majesty, shudderin'; 'we're terrible close; put a fire under the aft funnel at a' costs and get past as quick as we can.'

"It was pointed oot to his Majesty that the toon was evidently expectin' him, and so, to mak' things pleasant, he ordered the steam pinnace to land the week's washin' at the Charin' Cross o' the Hielan's—while the *Victoria and Albert* went on her way to Ballachulish."

X

HOW JINNET SAW THE KING

"I saw him and her on Thursday," said Erchie, "as nate's ye like, and it didna cost me mair than havin' my hair cut. They gaed past oor kirk, and the session put up a stand, and chairges ten shillin's a sate. 'Not for Joe,' said I; I'd sooner buy mysel' a new pair o' boots, and I went to Duffy and says I, 'Duffy, are ye no' gaun to hae oot yer bonny wee lorry at the heid o' Gairbraid Street and ask the wife and Jinnet and me to stand on't?'

'Right,' says Duffy, 'bring you Jinnet and I'll tak' my wife, and we'll hae a rale pant.'

"So there was the four o' us standin' five mortal 'oors on Duffy's coal-lorry. I was that gled when it was a' bye. But I'll wager there was naebody gledder than the King himsel', puir sowl! Frae the time he cam' into Gleska at Queen Street Station till the time he left Maryhill, he lifted his hat three million seven hundred and sixty-eight thousand and sixty-three times.

"Talk aboot it bein' a fine job bein' a King! I can tell ye the money's gey hard earned. Afore he starts oot to see his beloved people, he has to practise for a week wi' the dumb-bells, and feed himsel' up on Force, Grape-nuts, Plasmon, Pianolio, and a' thae strengthenin' diets that Sunny Jim eats.

"I thocht first Jinnet maybee wadna gang, her bein' in the Co-operative Store and no' awfu' ta'en up wi' Royalty, but, she jumped at the chance.

'The Queen's a rale nice buddy,' she says; 'no' that I'm personally acquainted wi' her, but I hear them sayin'. And she used to mak' a' her ain claes afore she mairried the King.'

"So Jinnet and me were oot on Duffy's lorry, sittin' on auld copies o' 'Reynolds' News,' and hurrayin' awa' like a pair o' young yins.

"The first thing Jinnet saw was a woman wi' a wean and its face no' richt washed.

'Fancy her bringin' oot her wean to see the King wi' a face like that,' says Jinnet, and gies the puir wee smout a sweetie.

"Frae that till it was time for us to gang hame Jinnet saw naething but weans, and her and Duffy's wife talked aboot weans even on. Ye wad think it was a baby-show we were at and no' a King's procession.

"Duffy sat wi' a Tontine face on him maist o' the time, but every

41

noo and then gaun up the street at the back o' us to buy himsel' a
bottle o' broon robin, for he couldna get near a pub; and I sat tryin'
as hard's I could to think hoo I wad like to be a King, and what kind
o' waistcoats I wad wear if I had the job. On every hand the flags
were wavin', and the folk were eatin' Abernaithy biscuits.

"At aboot twelve o'clock cannons begood to bang."

'Oh my! I hope there's nae weans near thae cannons or they micht
get hurt,' says Jinnet.

"Little did she think that at that parteecular meenute the King was
comin' doon the tunnel frae Cowlairs, and tellin' her Majesty no' to
be frichted.

"When the King set foot in the Queen Street Station he gied the
wan look roond him, and says he, 'Is this Gleska, can ony o' ye tell
me?'

'It is that, wi' your Majesty's gracious permission,' says the porter;
'sees a haud o' yer bag.'

'I mind fine o' bein' here yince afore,' says the King, and gangs
oot into George Square.

'Whitna graveyaird's this?' he asks, lookin' at the statues.

'It's no' a graveyaird; it's a square, and that's the Municeepal
Buildin',' somebody tells him. His Majesty then laid a foundation-
stone as smert's ye like wi' his least wee bit touch, and then went
into the Municeepal Buildin's and had a snack.

"He cam' oot feelin' fine. 'The Second City o' the Empire!' he
says. 'I can weel believ't. If it wasna for my business bein' in London
I wad hae a hoose here. Whit am I to dae next?'

"They took his Majesty doon Buchanan Street.

'No bad!' says he.

"Then he cam' to Argyle Street, and gaed west, past the
Hielan'man's Cross at the heid o' Jamaica Street. He sees a lot o'
chaps there wi' the heather stickin' oot o' their ears, and a tartan
brogue that thick it nearly spiled the procession."

'The Hielan'man's Cross,' says he: 'man, ay! I've heard o't.
Kamerhashendoo. If I had thocht o't I wad hae brocht my kilts and
my pibroch and a' that.'

"A' the wey doon the Dumbarton Road the folk were fair hingin'
oot o' their windows, wavin' onything at a' they could get a haud o',
and the Royal carriage was bump-bump-bumpin' like a' that ower the
granite setts."

'Whit's wrang wi' the streets o' Gleska?' says the King, him bein' used to wud streets in London, whaur he works.

'It's granite, if ye please,' says they.

'Oh ay!' says the King; 'man, it mak's a fine noise. Will we soon be there? I like this fine, but I wadna like to keep onybody waitin'.'

"At Finnieston the folk cam' up frae the side streets and fair grat wi' patriotic fervour. Forbye, a' the pubs were shut for an 'oor or twa."

'Whit I want to see's the poor,' says the King. 'I'm tired lookin' at the folk that's weel aff; they're faur ower common.'

'Them's the poor,' he was tellt; 'it's the best we can dae for your Majesty.'

'But they're awfu' bien-lookin' and weel put on,' says he.

'Oh ay!' they tells him, 'that's their Sunday claes.'

"And so the Royal procession passed on its way, the King being supplied wi' a new hat every ten minutes, to mak' up for the yins he spiled liftin' them to his frantic and patriotic subjects.

"In ten to fifteen minutes he examined the pictures in the Art Galleries—the Dutch, the English, the Italian, and the Gleska schools o' painters; the stuffed birds, and the sugaraully hats the polis used to hae when you and me was jinkin' them."

'Och, it's fine,' says he; 'there's naething wrang wi' the place. Are we no' near Maryhill noo?'

"Ye see his Majesty had on a bate he could see the hale o' Gleska in five 'oors or less, an' be oot sooner than ony ither king that ever set a fit in it. They wanted him to mak' a circular tour o't, and come back to the Municeepal Buildin's for his tea."

'Catch me,' says he. 'I'm gaun back to Dalkeith.'

"A' this time we were standin' on Duffy's lorry, flanked on the left by the Boys' Brigade, lookin' awfu' fierce, and the rifleman frae Dunoon on the richt. Every noo an' then a sodger went bye on a horse, or a lassie nearly fainted and had to be led alang the line by a polisman, and him no' awfu' carin' for the job. Duffy was gaun up the street to buy broon robin that aften he was gettin' sunburnt, and my wife Jinnet nearly hurt her een lookin' for weans."

'Look at thon wee wean, Erchie,' she wad aye be tellin' me,' does't no' put ye in mind o' Rubbert's wee Hughie? Oh, the cratur!'

'Wumman,' I tellt her, 'this is no a kinderspiel ye're at; it's a Royal procession. I wonder to me ye wad be wastin' yer e'esicht lookin' at weans when there's sae mony braw sodgers.'

'Oh, Erchie!' says she, 'I'm bye wi' the sodgers'; and jist wi' that the procession cam' up the street. First the Lancers wi' their dickies stickin' ootside their waistcoats.

'Man, them's fine horses,' says Duffy, wi' a professional eye on the beasts. 'Chaps me that broon yin wi the white feet.'

"Then cam' the King and Queen."

'Whaur's their croons?' asks Duffy's wife. 'I divna believe that's them at a'.'

'That's them, I'll bate ony money,' I says. 'Ye can tell by the hurry they're in.'

'Oh, the craturs!' says Jinnet, and then says she, 'Oh, Erchie! look at the wean hanging ower that window. I'm feart it'll fa' ower.'

"Afore she could get her een aff the wean the King's cairrage was past, and the rest o' the Lancers cam' clatterin' after them."

'Noo for the brass band!' says Duffy, lookin' doon the street. But there was nae brass bands. The show was bye.

'If I had kent that was to be a' that was in't, I wad never hae ta'en oot my lorry,' says Duffy, as angry as onything, and made a breenge for anither bottle o' broon robin.

'Och, it was fine,' says Jinnet. 'I never saw sae mony weans in a' my days.'

"And the crood began to scale.

"His Majesty reached Maryhill Station exact to the minute, wi' his eye on his watch."

'Weel, that's bye onywye,' says he, and somebody cries for a speech.

'People o' Gleska,' he says, 'I have seen your toon. It's fine— there's naething wrang wi't,' and then the gaird blew his whustle, and the train went aff.

"The great event was ower, the rain begood to fa' again; the Gilmorehill student hurried hame to blacken his face and put on his sister's frock. The coloured ping-pong balls strung ower Sauchieha' Street was lighted, the illuminated skoosh cars began to skoosh up and doon the street, the public-hooses did a fine tred."

'I'm gled it's a' bye,' says Jinnet, when we got hame to oor ain hoose.

'Indeed, and so am I,' Says I. 'There wad be fine fun in this warld a' the time if we werena' trying for't.'"

XI

ERCHIE RETURNS

For weeks I had not seen Erchie. He was not to be met on the accustomed streets, and St Kentigern's Kirk having been closed since July for alterations and repairs, it was useless to go there in search of its beadle. Once I met Duffy, and asked him what had become of the old man.

"Alloo you Erchie!" was all the information he would vouchsafe; "if he's keepin' oot o' sicht, he'll hae his ain reason for't. Mind, I'm no' sayin' onything against the cratur, though him and me's had mony a row. He's a' richt if ye tak' him the richt wye. But sly! He's that sly, the auld yin, ye can whiles see him winkin' awa' to himsel' ower something he kens that naebody else kens, and that he's no gaun to tell to them. I havena seen the auld fuiter since the Fair week. Perhaps he's gotten genteel and bidin' doon at Rothesay till the summer steamboats stop. There's yin thing sure—it's no' a case o' wife-desertion, for Jinnit's wi' him. I can tell by the venetian blinds and the handle o' their door. Sly! Did ye say sly? Man, it's no' the word for't. Erchie MacPherson's fair lost at the waitin'. He should hae been a poet, or a statesman, or something in the fancy line like that."

It was with the joy of a man who has made up his mind he has lost a sovereign and finds it weeks after in the lining of his waistcoat, I unexpectedly met Erchie on Saturday.

"Upon my word, old friend," I said, "I thought you were dead."

"No, nor deid!" retorted Erchie. "Catch me! I'm nane o' the deein' kind. But I micht nearly as weel be deid, for I've been thae twa months in Edinburgh. Yon's the place for a man in a decline. It's that slow he wad hae a chance o' livin' to a grand auld age. There's mair o' a bustle on the road to Sichthill Cemetery ony day in the week than there is in Princes Street on a Setturday nicht. I had a bit job there for the last ten weeks, and the only pleesure I had was gaun doon noo and then to the Waverley Station to see the bonny wee trains frae Gleska. They're a' richt for scenery and the like o' that in Edinburgh but they're no' smert."

"But it's an old saying, Erchie, that all the wise men in Glasgow come from the East—that's to say, they come from Edinburgh."

"Yes, and the wiser they are the quicker they come," said Erchie. "Man! and it's only an 'oor's journey, and to see the wye some o' them gae on bidin' ower yonder ye wad think they had the Atlantic Ocean to cross. There should be missionaries sent ower to Edinburgh explainin' things to the puir deluded craturs. Ony folk that wad put thon big humplock o' a hill they ca' the Castle in the middle o' the street, spilin' the view, and hing their washin's on hay-rakes stuck oot at their windows, hae muckle to learn."

"Still, I have no doubt Edinburgh's doing its best, Erchie," I said.

"Maybe, but they're no' smert; ye wad hae yer pouch picked half a dizzen times in Gleska in the time an Edinburgh polisman tak's to rub his een to waken himsel' when ye ask him the road to Leith.

"Did ye ever hear tell o' the Edinbugh man that ance ventured to Gleska and saw the hopper dredgers clawtin' up the glaur frae the Clyde at Broomielaw?

'Whit are ye standin' here for? Come awa' and hae a gless o' milk,' said a freen' to him.

'No,' said he, glowerin' like onything; 'I've coonted 364 o' thae wee buckets comin' oot the watter, and I'll no move a step oot o' here till I see the last o' them!'

"The puir cratur never saw a rale river in his life afore. Och! but Edinburgh's no' that bad; ye can aye be sure o' gettin' yer nicht's sleep in't at ony 'oor o' the day, it's that quate. They're aye braggin' that it's cleaner than Gleska, as if there was onything smert aboot that."

'There's naething dirtier than a dirty Gleska man,' said yin o' them to me ae day.

'There is,' says I.

'Whit?' says he.

'Twa clean Edinburgh yins,' says I.

'Och! but I'm only in fun. Edinburgh's a' richt; there's naething wrang wi' the place ance ye're in it if ye hae a book to read. I hate to hear the wye Duffy and some o' them speak aboot Edinburgh, the same as if it was shut up a'thegither. How wad we like it oorsel's? I hae maybe a flet fit, but I hae a warm hert, and I'll aye stick up for Edinburgh. I had an uncle that near got the jyle there for running ower yin o' their tramway caurs. They've no skoosh cars in Edinburgh, they're thon ither kin' that's pu'ed wi' a rope and wiles the rope breaks. But it doesna maitter, naebody's in ony hurry gaun to ony place in Edinburgh, and the passengers jist sit where they are till it's mended."

"Well, anyhow, Erchie, we're glad to see you back," I said.

"Gled to see me back!" he cried. "I'll wager ye didna ken I was awa', and the only folk that kent we werena in Gleska for the past twa or three months was the dairy and the wee shop we get oor vegetables frae.

"When I was in Edinburgh yonder, skliffin' alang the streets as fast's I could, and nippin' mysel' every noo and then to keep mysel' frae fa'in' asleep, I wad be thinkin' to mysel', 'How are they gettin' on in Gleska wantin' Erchie MacPherson? Noo that they've lost me, they'll ken the worth o' me.' I made shair that, at least, the skoosh cars wad hae to stop runnin' when I was awa', and that the polis band wad come doon to the station to meet me when I cam' hame.

"Dod! ye wad hardly believe it, but ever since I cam' back I meet naebody but folk that never ken't I was awa'. It's a gey hertless place Gleska that way. Noo, in Edinburgh it's different. They're gey sweart to lose ye in Edinburgh ance they get haud o' ye; that's the way they keep up the price o' the railway ticket to Gleska.

"I was tellin' Duffy aboot Edinburgh, and he's gaun through wi' a trip to see't on Monday. It'll be a puir holiday for the cratur, but let him jist tak' it. He'll be better there than wastin' his money in a toon. When Duffy goes onywhere on ony o' the Gleska holidays, it's generally to Airdrie, or Coatbrig, or Clydebank he goes, and walks aboot the streets till the polis put him on the last train hame for Gleska, and him singin' 'Dark Lochnagar' wi' the tears in his een.

"He'll say to me next morning,' 'Man! Erchie, thon's a thrivin' place, Coatbrig, but awfu' bad whisky.'

"There's a lot like him aboot a Gleska holiday. They'll be gettin' up to a late breakfast wi' no parridge till't on Monday mornin', and sayin,' 'Man! it's a grand day for Dunoon,' and then start druggin' themsel's wi' drams. Ye wad think they were gaun to get twa teeth ta'en oot instead o' gaun on a holiday.

"That's no' my notion o' a holiday, either in the Autumn or the Spring. I'm takin' Jinnet oot on Monday to Milliken Park to see her kizzen that keeps a gairden. We'll hae an awfu' wrastle in the mornin' catchin' the train, and it'll be that crooded we'll hae to stand a' the way. The wife's kizzen will be that gled to see us she'll mak' tea for us every half-oor and send oot each time to the grocer's for mair o' thon biled ham ye aye get at burials. I'll get my feet a' sair walkin' up and doon the gairden coontin' the wife's kizzen's aipples that's no' richt ripe yet, and Jinnet and me'll hae to cairry hame a big poke o' rhuburb or greens, or some ither stuff we're no wantin', and the train'll be an 'oor late gettin' into Gleska.

"That's a holiday. The only time ye enjoy a holiday is when it's
a' bye."

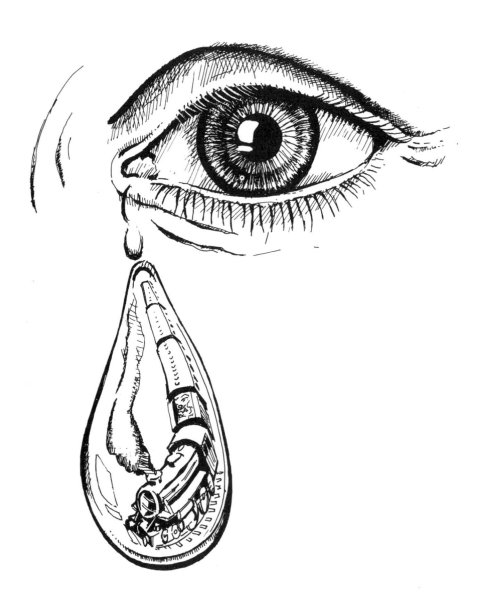

XII

DUFFY'S FIRST FAMILY

More than a year after the King's visit Erchie and I one day passed a piano-organ in the street playing "Dark Lochnagar." The air attracted him. He hummed it very much out of tune for some minutes after.

"Do ye hear that?" said he, "Dark Lochnagar. I used ance to could nearly play't on the mooth harmonium. I learned if aff Duffy. Him and me was mairried aboot the same time. We lived in the same close up in the Coocaddens—him on the top flet, and Jinnet and me in the flet below. Oor wifes had turn aboot o' the same credle—and it was kept gey throng, I'm tellin' ye. If it wasna Duffy up the stair at nicht, efter his wark was done, rockin' awa' wi' a grudge to the tune o' 'Dark Lochnagar,' it was me below at not 'Auld Lang Syne,' but yon ither yin ye ken fine. I daresay it was rockin' the credle helped to mak' my feet flet, and it micht hae happened in a far waur cause.

"It was Duffy's first wife; she dee'd, I think, to get rid o' him—the cratur! Duffy's yin o' thae men wi' a great big lump o' a hert that brocht the tear to his ain een when he was singin' 'Bonny Annie Laurie' doon in the Mull o' Kintyre Vaults, but wad see his wife to bleezes afore he wad brush his ain boots for Sunday, and her no' weel. She fair adored him, too. She thocht Duffy was jist the ordinar' kind o' man, and that I was a kind o' eccentric peely-wally sowl, because I sometimes dried the dishes, and didna noo' an then gie Jinnet a beltin'."

'His looks is the best o' him,' she wad tell Jinnet.

'Then' he's gey hard up!' I wad say to Jinnet when she tellt me this.

'He's no very strong,'—that was aye her cry, when she was fryin' anither pun' o' ham and a pair o' kippers for his breakfast.

"Duffy's first wean was Wullie John. Ye wad think, to hear Duffy brag aboot him, that it was a new patent kind o' wean, and there wasna anither in Coocaddens, whaur, I'm tellin' ye, weans is that rife ye hae to walk to yer work skliffin' yer feet in case ye tramp on them.

"Duffy's notion was to rear a race o' kind o' gladiators, and he rubbed him a' ower every nicht wi' olive-oil to mak' him soople. Nane o' your fancy foods for weans for Wullie John. It was rale auld

Caledonia parridge and soor dook. That soor the puir wee smout went aboot grewin' wi' its mooth a' slewed to the side, as if it was practising the wye the women haud their hairpins.

"Mony time I've seen oor Jinnet sneak him into oor hoose to gie him curds and cream. He said he liked them fine, because they were sae slippy."

'Show your temper, Wullie John,' Duffy wad tell him when onybody was in the hoose, and the wee cratur was trained at that to put on a fearfu' face and haud up his claws.

'See that!' Duffy wad say as prood as onything, 'the game's there, I'm tellin' ye.'

"Then Duffy began to harden him. He wad haud him up by the lug to see if he was game, and if he grat that was coonted wan to Duffy, and Wullie John got nae jeely on his piece. He was washed every mornin', winter and summer, in cauld watter in the jaw-box, and rubbed wi' a tooel as coorse as a carrot-grater till the skin was peelin' aff his back."

'Ye need to bring oot the glow,' Duffy wad say to me.

'If it gangs on much further,' I tellt him, 'I'll bring oot the polis.'

"Wullie John was fair on the road for bein' an A1 gladiator, but he went and dee'd on Duffy, and I never saw a man mair chawed.

"Duffy's next was a laddie too—they ca'd him Alexander. There was gaun to be nane o' their hardenin' dydoes wi' Alexander.

"It was aboot the time Duffy took to politics, and said the thing the Democratic pairty wanted was educated men wi' brains. He made up his mind that Alexander wad never cairry a coalpoke, but get the best o' learnin' if it cost a pound.

"He wasna very strong, was Alexander, and Duffy fed him maist o' the time on Gregory's mixture, cod-ile, and ony ither stuff he could buy by word o' mooth at the apothecary's withoot a doctor's line. Alexander was gettin medicine poored into him that often he was feared to gant in case he wad jar his teeth on a table-spoon when his een was shut. He wore hot-water bottles to his feet in the deid o' summer, and if he had a sair heid in the mornin' afore he started for the school on the geography days he was put to his bed and fed on tapioca. Everything went wrang wi' puir wee Alexander. The hives went in wi' him, and the dregs o' the measles cam' oot. He took every trouble that was gaun aboot except gymnastics. Duffy took him to Professor Coats, the bumpman, and had his heid examined. The Professor said it was as fine a heid o' its kind as ever he saw, and Duffy put a bawbee on the bag o' coals richt aff, and began to put the money bye for Alexander's college fees.

"Alexander's a man noo, and daein' fine. He's in the gas office. The only time he went to college was to read the meter there.

"Ye canna tell whit laddies 'll turn oot, and it's no' ony better wi' lassies. Duffy had a wheen o' lassies. I forget hoo mony there was a'thegither, but when they were coortin' ye was think ye were gaun doon the middle o' the Haymakers' country dance when ye cam' up the close at nicht.

"The auldest—she was Annie—was naething particular fancy. She jist nursed the rest, and made their peenies, and washed for them, and trimmed her ain hats, and made Duffy's auld waistcoats into suits for the wee yins, and never got to the dancin', so naebody married her, and she's there yet.

"A' the chaps cam' efter her sisters.

"The sisters never let on aboot the coal-ree and Duffy's lorry, but said their paw was in the coal tred—a kind o' a coal-maister. It was a bonny sicht to see them merchin' oot to their cookery lessons in the efternoons, their hair as curly's onything, and their beds no' made.

"The days they tried new dishes frae the cookery lessons at hame, Duffy took his meat in the Western Cookin' Depot, and cam' hame when it was dark. Yin o' them played the mandoline. The mandoline's a noble instrument. It cheers the workman's hame. A lassie gaun alang the street wi' a nice print dress, and a case wi' a mandoline, is jist the sort I wad fancy mysel' if I was a young yin and there wasna Jinnet. A fruiterer married the mandoline. The nicht she was merrit, Duffy sang 'Dark Lochnagar,' and winked at me like a' that."

'Learn your dochters the mandoline, Erchie,' says he in my lug, 'and they'll gang aff your haunds like snaw aff a dyke. That's the advice I wad gie ye if ye had ony dochters left. I wad hae made it the piano, but we couldna get a piano up past the bend on the stair.'

"Efter the mandoline went, the boys begood to scramble for Duffy's dochters as if they were bowl-money. The close-mooth was never clear o' cabs, and the rice was always up to your ankles on the stair. Duffy sang 'Dark Lochnagar' even-on, and aye kept winkin' at me."

'That's the mandoline awa',' says he, 'and the scientific dressmakin', and the shorthand, and the 'Curfew must not Ring Tonight,' and the revival meetin's, and the no' very weel yin that needs a quate hame. They're a' gane, Erchie, and I'm no' gien jeely-dishes awa' wi' them either. I'm my lee-lane, me and Annie. If ony o' thae chaps cam' efter Annie, I wad chase him doon the stair.'

'Man! Duffy,' I says to him, 'ye're selfish enough workin' aff a' them ornamental dochters on the young men o' Gleska that did ye nae hairm, and keepin' the best o' the hale jingbang in the hoose a' the time in case they see her.'

'Let them tak' it!' says Duffy, 'I'm no' a bit vexed for them,' and he started to sing 'Dark Lochnagar' as lood as ever, while Annie was puttin' on his boots.

"That was in Duffy's auld days. He married a second wife, and it was a fair tak'-in, for he thocht a wee green-grocer's shop she had was her ain, and a' the time it was her brither's."

'That's the mandoline for you, Duffy,' says I, when he tellt me.

"But that yin died on him too. She died last Mertinmas. Duffy's kind o' oot o' wifes the noo. And the warst o't is that his dochter Annie's gettin' married."

XIII

ERCHIE GOES TO A BAZAAR

There was a very self-conscious look on Erchie's face on Saturday when I met him with a hand-painted drain-pipe of the most generous proportions under his arm.

"It's aye the way," said he. "Did ye ever hae ony o' yer parteecular freen's meet ye when ye were takin' hame a brace o' grouse? No' a bit o' ye! But if it's a poke o' onything, or a parcel frae the country, whaur they havena ony broon paper, but jist 'The Weekly Mail,' and nae richt twine, ye'll no' can gang the length o' the street without comin' across everybody that gangs to yer kirk."

He put the drain-pipe down on the pavement—it was the evening—and sat on the end of it.

"So you are the latest victim to the art movement, Erchie?" I said. "You will be putting away your haircloth chairs and introducing the sticky plush variety. I was suspicious of that new dado in your parlour the day we had the tousy tea after Big Macphee's burial."

"Catch me!" said Erchie. "Them and their art! I wadna be encouragin' the deevils. If ye want to ken the way I'm gaun hame wi' this wally umbrella-staun', I'll tell ye the rale truth. It's jist this, that Jinnet's doon yonder at the Freemasons' Bazaar wi' red-hot money in her pooch, and canna get awa' till it's done. She's bocht a tea-cosy besides this drain-pipe, and a toaster wi' puce ribbons on't for haudin' letters and papers, and she'll be in luck for yince if she disna win the raffle for the lady's bicycle that she had twa tickets for. Fancy me oot in Grove Street in the early mornin' learnin' Jinnet the bicycle, and her the granny o' seeven!

"Of course, Jinnet's no' needin' ony bicycle ony mair than she's needin' a bassinette, but she has a saft hert and canna say no unless she's awfu' angry, and a young chap, speakin' awfu' Englified, wi' his hair a' vasaline, got roond her. She's waitin' behin' there to see if she wins the raffle, and to pick up ony bargains just a wee while afore the place shuts up—the rale time for bazaar bargains if ye divna get yer leg broken in the crush. I only went there mysel' to see if I could get her to come hame as lang as she had enough left to pay her fare on the skoosh car, but I micht as weel speak to the wind. She was fair raised ower a bargain in rabbits. It's an awfu' thing when yer wife tak's to bazaars. It's waur than drink.

"It's a female complaint. Ye'll no' find mony men bothered wi't unless they happen to be ministers. Ye'll no' see Duffy sittin' late at nicht knittin' wee bootees for weans they'll never in the warld fit, nor crochetin' doyleys, to aid the fund o' the Celtic Fitba' Club. Ye micht watch a lang while afore ye wad see me makin' tinsey 'ool ornaments wi' paste-heided preens for hingin' up in the best room o' dacent folk that never did me ony hairm.

"There wad be nae such thing as bazaars if there werena ony weemen. In thoosands o' weel-daein' hames in this Christian toon o' Gleska there's weemen at this very meenute neglectin' their men's suppers to sit doon and think as hard's they can whit they can mak' wi' a cut and a half o' three-ply fingerin' worsted, that'll no' be ony use to ony body, but'll look worth eighteenpence in a bazaar. If ye miss your lum hat, and canna find it to gang to a funeral, ye may be shair it was cut in scollops a' roond the rim and covered wi' velvet, and that wee Jeenie pented floores on't in her ain time to gie't the richt feenish for bein' an Art work-basket at yer wife's stall in some bazaar.

"Maist weemen start it withoot meanin' ony hairm, maybe wi' a table-centre, or a lamp-shade, or a pair o' bedroom slippers. There's no' much wrang wi' that; but it's a beginnin', and the habit grows on them till they're scoorin' the country lookin' for a chance to contribute whit they ca' Work to kirk bazaars and ony ither kinds o' bazaars that's handy. It mak's my hert sair sometimes to see weel-put-on-weemen wi' men o' their ain and dacent faimilies, comin' hame through back-streets staggerin' wi' parcels o' remnants for dressin' dolls or makin' cushions wi'. They'll hide it frae their men as long as they can, and then, when they're found oot, they'll brazen it oot and deny that it's ony great hairm.

"That's wan way the trouble shows itsel'.

"There's ither weemen—maistly younger and no' mairried—that's dyin' for a chance to be assistant stall-keepers, and wear white keps and aiprons, jist like tablemaids.

"That's the kind I'm feared for, and I'm nae chicken.

"When they see a man come into the bazaar and nae wife wi' him to tak' care o' him, they come swoopin' doon on him, gie him ony amount o' cleck, jist for fun, and ripe his pooches before he can button his jaicket.

"I'm no' sayin' they put their hands in his pooches, but jist as bad. They look that nice, and sae fond o' his tie and the way he has o' wearin' his moustache, that he's kittley doon to the soles o' his feet,

and wad buy a steam road-roller frae them if he had the money for't.
But they're no' sellin' steam road-rollers, the craturs! They're sellin'
shillin' dolls at twa-and-six that can open and shut their een, and say
'Maw' and 'Paw.' They're sellin carpet slippers, or bonny wee
bunches o' flooers, or raffle tickets for a rale heliotrope Persian cat.
It's the flyest game I ken. When that puir sowl gets oot o' the place
wi' naething in his pooches but his hands, and a dazed look in his
een, the only thing he can mind is that she said her name was Maud,
and that her hair was crimp, and that she didna put a preen in his
coat lapelle when she was puttin' the shillin' rose there, because she
said a preen wad cut love. She said that to every customer she had
for her flooers that day, wi' a quick look up in their face, and then
droppin' her eyes confused like, and her face red, and a' the time,
her, as like as no', engaged to a man.

"I wonder hoo it wad dae to hae a man's bazaar? They ocht to
have made the Freemasons' bazaar a man's yin, seein' the
Freemasons 'll no tell the weemen their secrets nor let them into
their lodges.

"A man's bazaar wad be a rale divert. Naethin' to be sold in't but
things for use, like meerschaum pipes, and kahootchy collars, and sox
the richt size, and chairs, and tables, and concertinas—everything
guaranteed to be made by men and them tryin'.

"The stalls wad be kept by a' the baronets that could be scraped
thegither and could be trusted withoot cash registers, and the stall
assistants wad be the pick o' the best-lookin' men in the toon—if ye
could get them sober enough. If Jinnet wad let me, I wad be willin'
to gie a hand mysel', for though I've a flet fit I've a warm hert, I'm
tellin' ye.

"I think I see Duffy walkin' roond the St Andrew's Hall, and it
got up to look like the Fall o' Babylon, tryin' to sell bunches o'
flooers. Dae ye think he wad sell mony to the young chaps like whit
Maud riped? Nae fears! He wad hae to tak' every customer oot and
stand him a drink afore he wad get a flooer aff his hands.

"Can ye fancy Duffy gaun roond tryin' to sell tickets for a raffle
o' a canary in a cage?"

'Here ye are, chaps and cairters! the chance o' yer lives for a
graund whustler, and no' ill to feed!'

"Na, na! a man o' the Duffy stamp wad be nae use for a bazaar,
even wi' a dress suit on and his face washed. It wad need young
stockbrokers, and chaps wi' the richt kind o' claes, wi' a crease doon

the front o' their breeks—Grosvenor Restaurant chaps, wi' the smell o' cigars aff their topcoats, and either ca'd Fred or Vincent. Then ye micht see that the ither sex that hiv a' the best o't wi' bazaars, the wye they're managed noo, wad flock to the man's bazaar and buy like onything. And maybe no'."

Erchie rose off the drain-pipe, and prepared to resume his way home with that ingenious object that proves how the lowliest things of life may be made dignified and beautiful—if fashion says they are so.

"Well, good night, old friend," I said. "I hope Mrs MacPherson will be lucky and get the bicycle."

"Dae ye, indeed?" said he. "Then ye're nae freen' o' mine. We're faur mair in the need o' a mangle."

"Then you can exchange for one."

"I'm no' that shair. Did I ever tell ye I ance won a pony in a raffle? It was at the bazaar oor kirk had in Dr Jardine's time when they got the organ. It was helpin' at the buffet, and I think they micht hae left me alane, me no' bein' there for fun, but at my tred, but wha cam' cravin' me to buy a ticket aff her but the doctor's guid-sister."

'There's three prizes,' says she; 'a pony wi' broon harness, a marble nock, and a dizzen knifes and forks.'

'I wad maybe risk it if it wisna for the pony,' I tellt her; 'I havena kep' a coachman for years, and I'm oot o' the way o' drivin' mysel'.'

'Oh! ye needna be that feared, ye'll maybe no' get the pony,' said she, and I went awa' like a fool and took the ticket.

"The draw took place jist when the bazaar was shuttin' on the Setturday nicht. And I won the pony wi' the broon harness.

"I tore my ticket and threeped it was a mistake, but I couldna get oot o't; they a' kent the pony was mine.

"It was stabled behind the bazaar, and had to be ta'en awa' that nicht. I offered it to onybody that wanted it for naething, but naebody wad tak' it aff my hands because they a' said they had to tak' the car hame, and they wadna be allooed to tak' a pony into a car wi' them. So they left me wi' a bonny-like prize.

"I put its claes on the best way I could, fanklin' a' the straps, and dragged it hame. We lived in the close at the time, and I thocht maybe Jinnet wad let me keep it in the lobby till the Monday mornin' till I could see whit I could dae. But she wadna hear tell o't. She said it wad scrape a' the waxcloth wi' its iron boots, and wad be a bonny-like thing to be nicherrin' a' Sunday, scandalisin' the neebours, forbye there bein' nae gress in the hoose to feed it on. I said I wad rise early in the mornin' and gaither dentylions for't oot at the Three-Tree Well, but she wadna let me nor the pony inside the door.

"It wasna an awfu' big broad pony, but a wee smout o' a thing they ca' a Shetland-shawl pony, and its harness didna fit it ony place at a'. It looked at the twa o' us, kind o' dazed like."

'Ye're no' gaun to turn my hoose into a stable, and me jist cleaned it this very day,' said Jinnet.

'And am I gaun to walk the streets a' nicht wi't?' I asked, near greetin'.

'Put it oot in the ash-pit, and the scavengers 'll tak' it awa' in the mornin',' she said, and I did that, forgettin' that the mornin' was the Sunday.

"But it didna maitter. The pony wasna there in the mornin', and I took guid care no' to ask for't."

XIV

HOLIDAYS

"Well, Erchie, not away on the Fair holidays?" I asked the old man one July day on meeting him as he came out of a little grocer's shop in the New City Road. The dignity of his profession is ever dear to Erchie. He kept his purchase behind his back, but I saw later it was kindling material for the morning fire.

"Not me!" said he. "There's nae Fair holidays for puir auld Erchie, no' even on the Sunday, or I might hae ta'en the skoosh car doon the wye o' Yoker, noo that a hurl on Sunday's no' that awfu' sair looked down on, or the 'Mornin' Star' bus to Paisley. But Jinnet went awa' on Setturday wi' her guid-sister to Dunoon, and I'm my lee-lane in the hoose till the morn's mornin'. It's nae divert, I'm tellin' ye. There's a lot o' things to mind forbye the windin' o' the nock on Setturday and watering the fuchsia. I can wait a municeepal banquet wi' ony man in my tred, but I'm no' great hand at cookin' for mysel'.

"Did I ever tell ye aboot the time the wife was awa' afore at a Fair, and I took a notion o' a seed-cake Duffy's first wife had to the tea she trated me to on the Sabbath?"

'It's as easy to mak' as boilin' an egg,' says Mrs Duffy, and gied me the recipe for't on condeetion that when I made it I was to bring her a sample. Something went wrong, and I brought her the sample next day in a bottle. It was a gey damp seedcake thon!

"I havena been awa' at a Fair mysel' since aboot the time Wullie was in the Foondry Boys, and used to gang to the Hielan's. I mind o't fine. Nooadays, in oor hoose, ye wad never jalouse it was the Fair at a' if it wasna for nae parridge in the mornin's.

"Ye'll hae noticed, maybe, that though we're a' fearfu' fond o' oor parridge in Scotland, and some men mak' a brag o' takin' them every mornin' just as if they were a cauld bath, we're gey gled to skip them at a holiday and just be daein' wi' ham and eggs.

"But in thae days, as I was sayin', the Fair was something like the thing. There was Mumford's and Glenroy's shows, and if ye hadna the money to get in, ye could aye pap eggs at the musicianers playing on the ootside, and the thing was as broad as it was lang. Forbye, ye didna get the name o' bein' keen on the theatricals if your faither was parteecular.

"I mind ance I hit a skeely-e'ed trombone player wi' an egg at

Vinegar Hill. The glee pairty—as ye might ca' him if ye were funny—chased me as far doon as the Wee Doo Hill. I could rin in thae days. Noo I've ower flet feet, though I've a warm hert too, I'm tellin' ye.

"If ye werena at the Shows in thae days ye went a trip wi' the steamer *Bonnie Doon*, and ye had an awfu' fine time o't on the Setturday if ye could jist mind aboot it on the Sunday morning'.

Duffy's gey coorse, bein' in the retail coal trade and cryin' for himsel', I'm no' like that at a' mysel'; it widna dae, and me in the poseetion. But I mind aince o' Duffy tellin' me he could never fa' asleep at the Fair Time till his wife gave him the idea o' lyin' on his left side, and coontin', yin by yin, a' the drams he had the night afore. He said it worked on him like chloryform.

"I hope ye'll no' mind me speakin' aboot drink. It's awfu' vulgar coonted noo, I hear, to let on ye ever heard that folk tak' it, but in thae days there was an awfu' lot o't partaken aboot Gleska. I'm tellt noo it's gaen clean oot o' fashion, and stane ginger's a' the go, and I see in the papers every Monday efter the Fair Setturday that 'there has been a gratifying decrease in the number o' cases at the Central Police Court compared wi' last year.' I'm that gled! I have been seein' that bit o' news in the papers for the last thirty years, and I hae nae doot that, in a year or twa, drunks and disorderlies 'll be sae scarce in Gleska at the Fair, the polis 'll hae to gang huntin' for them wi' bloodhounds.

"It's a fine thing the Press. It's aye keen to keep oor herts up. Ye'll notice, perhaps, that at every Gleska holiday the papers aye say the croods that left the stations were unprecedented. They were never kent to be ony ither wye.

"I daursay it's true enough. I went doon to the Broomielaw on Setturday to see Jinnet aff, and the croods on the Irish and Hielan' boats was that awfu', the men at the steerage end hadna room to pu' oot their pocket-handkies if they needed them. It's lucky they could dae withoot. When the butter-and-egg boats for Belfast and 'Derry left the quay, the pursers had a' to have on twa watches—at least they had the twa watch-chains, ane on each side, for fear the steamer wad capsize. I says to mysel', 'It's a peety a lot o' thae folk for Clachnacudden and County Doon dinna lose their return tickets and bide awa' when they're at it. Gleska's a fine toon, but jist a wee bit ower crooded nooadays.'

"I hae nae great notion for doon the watter mysel' at the Fair. Jinnet jist goes and says she'll tell me whit it's like. Whit she likes it for is that ye're never lonely.

"And it's that homely doon aboot Rothesay and Dunoon, wi' the Gleska wifes hangin' ower the windows tryin' as hard as they can to see the scenery, between the whiles they're fryin' herrin' for Wull. And then there's wee Hughie awfu' ill wi' eatin' ower mony hairy grossets.

"But it's fine for the weans, too, to be gaun sclimbin' aboot the braes pu'in' the daisies and the dockens and the dentylions and–and– and a' thae kin' o' flooers ye'll can touch withoot onybody findin' fault wi' ye. It's better for the puir wee smouts than moshy in the back-coort, and puttin' bunnets doon the stanks. They'll mind it a' their days—the flooers and the dulse for naething, and the grossets and the Gregory's mixture. It's Nature. It's the Rale Oreeginal.

"It does the wife a lot o' guid to gae doon the watter at the Fair. She's that thrang when she's at hame she hasna had time yet to try a new shooglin'-chair we got at the flittin'. But 'it's a rest,' she'll say when she comes back, a' moth-eaten wi' the midges. And then she'll say, 'I'm that gled it's ower for the year.'

"That's the droll thing aboot the Fair and the New Year; ye're aye in the notion that somethin' awfu' nice is gaun to happen, and naethin' happens at a', unless it's that ye get your hand awfu' sair hashed pu'in' the cork oot o' a bottle o' beer."

"You'll be glad, I'm sure, to have the goodwife back, Erchie?" I said, with an eye on the fire-kindlers.

He betrayed some confusion at being discovered, and then laughed.

"Ye see I've been for sticks," said he. "That's a sample o' my hoose-keepin'. I kent there was something parteecular to get on the Setturday night, and thought it was pipeclay. The grocer in there wad be thinkin' I was awa' on the ping-pong if he didna ken I was a beadle. Will ye be puttin' ony o' this bit crack in the papers?"

"Well, I don't know, Erchie; I hope you won't mind if I do."

"Oh! I'm no heedin'. It's a' yin to Erchie, and does nae hairm to my repitation, though I think sometimes your spellin's a wee aff the plumb. Ye can say that I said keepin' a hoose is like ridin' the bicycle; ye think it's awfu' easy till ye try't."

"That's a very old discovery, Erchie. I fail to understand why you should be anxious to have it published now."

Erchie winked. "I ken fine whit I'm aboot," said he. "It'll please the leddies to ken that Erchie said it, and I like fine to be popular.

My private opeenion is that a man could keep a hoose as weel as
a woman ony day if he could only bring his mind doon to't."

XV

THE STUDENT LODGER

It was with genuine astonishment Erchie one day had his wife come to him with a proposal that she should keep a lodger.

"A ludger!" he cried. "It wad be mair like the thing if ye keepit a servant lassie, for whiles I think ye're fair wrocht aff yer feet."

"Oh, I'm no' sae faur done as a' that," said Jinnet. "I'm shair I'm jist as smert on my feet as ever I was, and I could be daein' wi' a ludger fine. It was keep me frae wearyin'."

"Wearyin'!" said her husband. "It's comin' to't when my ain wife tells me I'm no' company for her. Whit is't ye're wantin', and I'll see whit I can dae. If it's music ye're for, I'll buy a melodian and play't every nicht efter my tea. If it's improvin' conversation ye feel the want o', I'll ask Duffy up every ither nicht and we'll can argue on Fore Ordination and the chance o' the Celtic Fitba' Club to win the League Championship the time ye're darnin' stockin's. 'Wearyin'' says she! Perhaps ye wad like to jine a dancin' school. Weel, I'll no' hinder ye, I'm shair, but I'll no promise to walk to the hall wi' ye every nicht cairryin' yer slippers. Start a ludger! I'm shair we're no' that hard up!"

"No, we're no' that hard up," Jinnet confessed, "but for a' the use we mak' o' the room we micht hae somebody in it, and it wad jist be found money. I was jist thinkin' it wad be kind o' cheery to have a dacent young chap gaun oot and in. I'm no' for ony weemen ludgers. They're jist a fair bother, aye hingin' aboot the hoose and puttin' their nose into the kitchen, tellin' ye the richt wye to dae this and that, and burnin' coal and gas the time a man ludger wad be oot takin' the air."

"Takin' drink, mair likely," said Erchie, "and comin' hame singin' 'Sodgers o' the Queen,' and scandalisin' the hale stair."

"And I'm no' for a tredsman," Jinnet went on, with the air of one whose plans were all made.

"Of course no'," said her husband, "tredsmen's low. They've no' cless. It's a peety ye mairried yin. Perhaps ye're thinkin' o' takin' in a Chartered Accoontant, or maybe a polisman. Weel I'm jist tellin' ye I wadna hae a polisman in my paurlor. His helmet wadna gang richt wi' the furniture, and the blecknin' for his boots wad cost ye mair than whit he paid for his room."

"No, nor a polisman!" said Jinnet. "I was thinkin' o' maybe a quate lad in a warehouse, or a nice factor's clerk, or something o' that sort. He wad be nae bother. It's just the ae makin' o' parridge in the mornin'. Ye're no' to thraw wi' me aboot this, Erchie; my mind's made up I'm gaun to keep a ludger."

"If your mind's made up," he replied, "then there's nae use o' me argy-bargyin' wi' ye. I'm only your man. It bates me to ken whit ye're gaun to dae wi' the money, if it's no' to buy a motor-cairrage. Gie me your word ye're no' gaun in for ony sports o' that kind. I wad hate to see ony wife o' mine gaun skooshin' oot the Great Western Road on a machine like a tar-biler, wi' goggles on her een and a kahootchy trumpet skriechin' 'pip! pip!'"

"Ye're jist an auld haver," said Jinnet, and turned to her sewing, her point gained.

★　　★　　★

A fortnight after, as a result of a ticket with the legend 'Apartments' in the parlour window, Jinnet was able to meet her husband's return to tea one night with the announcement that she had got a lodger. "A rale gentleman!" she explained. "That weel put-on! wi' twa Gledstone bags, yin o' them carpet, and an alerm clock for waukenin' him in the mornin'. He cam' this efternoon in a cab, and I think he'll be easy put up wi' and tak' jist whit we tak' oorsel's."

"I hope he's no' a theatrical," said Erchie. "Me bein' a beadle in a kirk it wadna be becomin' to hae a theatrical for a ludger. Forbye, they never rise oot o' their beds on the Sunday, but lie there drinkin' porter and readin' whit the papers say aboot their play actin'."

"No, nor a theatrical!" cried Jinnet. "I wadna mak' a show o' my hoose for ony o' them. It's a rale nice wee fair-heided student."

Erchie threw up his hands in amazement. "Michty me!" said he, "a student. Ye micht as weel hae taen in a brass baun' or the Cairter's Trip when ye were at it. Dae ye ken whit students is, Jinnet? I ken them fine, though I was never at the college mysel', but yince I was engaged to hand roond beer at whit they ca'd a Gaudiamus. Ye have only to tak' the mildest wee laddie that has bad e'e-sicht and subject to sair heids frae the country and mak' a student o' him to rouse the warst passions o' his nature. His mither, far awa' in Clachnacudden, thinks he's hurtin' his health wi' ower muckle study, but the only hairm he's daein' himsel' is to crack his voice cryin' oot impidence to his professors. I'm vexed it's a student, and a fair-heided yin at that, I've noticed that the fair-heided yins were aye the warst."

Weel, he's there onywye, and we'll jist hae to mak' the best we can wi' him," said Jinnet. "Forbye, I think he's a guid-leevin' lad, Erchie. He tellt me he was comin' oot for a minister."

"Comin' oot for a minister!" said Erchie. "Then that's the last straw! I'm sorry for your chevalier and book-case; he'll be sclimbin' int't some nicht thinkin' it's the concealed bed."

The room door opened, a voice bawled in the lobby, "Mrs MacPherson, hey! Mrs MacPherson," and the student, without waiting his landlady's appearance, walked coolly into the kitchen.

"Hulloo! old chap, how's biz?" he said to Erchie, and seated himself airily on the table, with a pipe in his mouth. He was a lad of twenty, with spectacles.

"I canna complain," said Erchie. "I hope ye're makin' yersel' at hame."

"Allow me for that!" said the student.

"That's nice," said Erchie, blandly. "See and no' be ower blate, and if there's onything ye're wantin' that we havena got, we'll get it for ye. Ye'll no' know whit ye need till ye see whit ye require. It's a prood day for us to hae a diveenity student in oor room. If we had expected it we wad hae had a harmonium."

"Never mind the harmonium," said the student. "For music lean on me, George P. Tod. I sing from morn till dewy eve. When I get up in the morning, jocund day stands on the misty mountain top, and I give weight away to the bloomin' lark. Shakespeare, Mr MacPherson. The Swan of Avon. He wrote a fairly good play. What I wanted to know was if by any chance Mrs MacPherson was a weepist?"

"Sir?" said Jinnet.

"Do you, by any chance, let the tear doon fa'?"

"Not me!" said Jinnet, "I'm a cheery wee woman."

"Good!" said Tod. "Then you're lucky to secure a sympathetic and desirable lodger. To be gay is my forte. The last landlady I had was thrice a widow. She shed the tears of unavailing regret into my lacteal nourishment with the aid of a filler, I think, and the milk got thinner and thinner. I was compelled at last to fold my tent like the justly celebrated Arabs of song and silently steal away. 'Why weep ye by the tide, ladye?' I said to her, 'If it were by the pint I should not care so much, but methinks your lachrymal ducts are too much on the hair-trigger.' It was no use, she could not help it, and—in short, here I am."

"I'm shair we'll dae whit we can for ye," said Jinnet. "I never had a ludger before."

"So much the better," said George Tod. "I'm delighted to be the object of experiment—the *corpus vile*, as we say in the classics, Mr MacPherson—and you will learn a good deal with me. I will now proceed to burn the essential midnight oil. Ah, thought, thought! You little know, Mr MacPherson, the weary hours of study——"

"It's no' ile we hae in the room, it's gas," said Erchie. "But if ye wad raither hae ile, say the word and we'll get it for ye."

"Gas will do," said the student; "it is equally conducive to study, and more popular in all great congeries of thought."

"When dae ye rise in the mornin', Mr Tod?" asked Jinnet. "I wad like to ken when I should hae your breakfast ready."

"Rise!" said Tod. "Oh, any time! 'When the morn, with russet mantle clad, walks o'er the dew on yon high eastern hill.'"

"Is't Garnethill or Gilshochill?" said Erchie, anxiously. "I wad rise mysel', early in the mornin', and gang oot to whichever o' them it is to see the first meenute the dew comes, so that ye wadna lose ony time in gettin' up and started wi' your wark."

The lodger for the first time looked at his landlord with a suspicious eye. He had a faint fear that the old man might be chaffing him, but the innocence of Erchie's face restored his perkiness.

"I was only quoting the bard," he explained, as he left the kitchen. "Strictly speaking, the morn with russet mantle clad can go to the deuce for me, for I have an alarm clock. Do not be startled if you hear it in the morning. It goes off with incredible animation."

★   ★   ★

"Oh, Erchie, isn't he nice?" said Jinnet, when the lodger had withdrawn. "That smert, and aye talks that jovial, wi' a lot o' words I canna mak' heid nor tail o'."

"Erchie filled his pipe and thought a little, "Smert's the word Jinnet," said he. "That's whit students is for."

"I don't think he's very strong." said Jinnet. "If he was in his mither's hoose she wad be giein' him hough soup for his dinner. I think I'll jist mak' some for him to-morrow, and put a hot-water bottle in his bed."

"That's richt," said Erchie; "and if ye hae a haddie or a kippered herrin', or onything else handy, it'll dae for me."

"Ye're jist a haver!" said Jinnet.

For a week George P. Tod was a model lodger. He came in at early hours of the evening and went to bed timeously, and was no great trouble to his landlady, whose cookery exploits in his interest were a great improvement on anything he had ever experienced in lodgings before.

When he was in his room in the evenings Jinnet insisted on the utmost quietness on the part of her husband. "Mr Tod's at his hame lessons," she would say. "It'll no' dae to disturb him. Oh, that heid wark! that heid wark! It must be an awfu' thing to hae to be thinkin' even-on."

"Heid wark?" said her husband. "I ken the heid wark he's like enough at. He's learnin' the words o' 'Mush Mush, tu-ral-i-ady' to sing at the students' procession, or he's busy wi' a dictionary writin' hame to his paw to send him a post office order for twa pounds to jine the Y.M.C.A. But he's no' thinkin' o' jinin' the Y.M.C.A.; he's mair likely to start takin' lessons at a boxin' cless."

But even Erchie was compelled to admit that the lad was no unsatisfactory lodger.

"I declare, Jinnet," he said, "I think he's yin o' the kind o' students ye read aboot but very seldom see. His faither 'll be a wee fairmer up aboot Clachnacudden, hainin' a' the money he can, and no' giein' his wife her richt meat, that he may see his son through the college and waggin' his heid in a pulpit. Him and his faither's the stuff they mak' the six shillin' Scotch novells oot o'—the kind ye greet at frae the very start—for ye ken the puir lad, that was aye that smert in the school, and won a' the bursaries, is gaun to dee in the last chapter wi' a decline."

"Puir things," said Jinnet.

"Ye divna see ony signs o' decline aboot Mr Tod, do ye?" asked Erchie, anxiously.

"I didna notice," replied Jinnet, "but he tak's his meat weel enough."

"The meat's the main thing! But watch you if he hasna a hoast and thon hectic flush that aye breaks oot in chapter nine jist aboot the time he wins the gold medal."

"Och, ye're jist an auld haver, Erchie," said the wife. "Ye're no' to be frichtenin' me aboot the puir callant, jist the same age as oor

66

ain Willie."

The time of the Rectorial Election approached, and Tod began to display some erratic habits. It was sometimes the small hours of the morning before he came home, and though he had a latch-key, Jinnet could never go to bed until her lodger was in for the night. Sometimes she went out to the close-mouth to look if he might be comin, and the first night that Erchie, coming home late from working at a civic banquet, found her there, Tod narrowly escaped being told to take his two bags and his alarm clock elsewhere.

"I was needin' a moothfu' o' fresh air onywye," was Jinnet's excuse for being out at such an hour. "But I'm feared that puir lad's workin' himsel' to death."

"Whaur dae ye think he's toilin'?" asked her husband.

"At the nicht-school," said Jinnet. "I'm shair the college through the day's plenty for him."

"The nicht-school!" cried Erchie. "Bonny on the nicht-school! He's mair likely to be roond in Gibson Street batterin' in the doors o' the Conservative committee-rooms, for I ken by his specs and his plush weskit he's a Leeberal. Come awa' in to your bed and never mind him. Ye wad be daein' him a better turn maybe if ye chairged the gazogene to be ready for the mornin', when he'll be badly wantin't, if I'm no' faur mistaken."

Erchie was right—the gazogene would have been welcome next morning. As it was, the lodger was indifferent to breakfast, and expressed an ardent desire for Health Salts.

Erchie took them in to him, and found him groaning with a headache.

"The dew's awfu' late on the high eastern hills this mornin', Mr Tod," said Erchie. "Losh, ye're as gash as the Laird o' Garscadden! I'm feart ye're studyin' far ower hard. It's no' for the young and growin' to be hurtin' their heids wi' nicht-schools and day-schools. Ye would whiles tak' a bit rest to yersel'. And no' a bit o' yer breakfast touched! Mrs MacPherson 'll no' be the pleased woman wi' ye this day, I can tell ye!"

Tod looked up with a lack-lustre eye. "Thought, Mr MacPherson, thought!" said he. "Hard, incessant, braincorroding thought! In the words of the Bard of Avon, 'He who increaseth knowledge increaseth sorrow.'"

"I aye thocht that was 'Ecclesiastes,' Mr Tod," said Erchie, meekly.

"In a way, yes," hastily admitted Tod. "It *was* 'Ecclesiastes,' as you say, but Shakespeare had pretty much the same idea. You will find it in—in—in his plays."

That afternoon began the more serious of Jinnet's experiences of divinity students. Nine young gentlemen with thick walking-sticks visited Tod's apartment *en masse*. The strains of "Mush Mush, tu-ral-i-ady," bellowed inharmoniously by ten voices, and accompanied by the beating of the walking-sticks on the floor, kept a crowd of children round the close-mouth for hours, and somewhat impeded the ordinary traffic of the street.

"There must be a spree on in auld MacPherson's," said the tenement. When Erchie came home he found Jinnet distracted. "Oh, whit a day I've had wi' them students!" she wailed.

"But look at the money ye're makin' aff your room," said her husband. "Wi' whit ye get frae Tod, ye'll soon hae enough for the motor cairrage and a yacht forbye."

"I'm feart to tell ye, Erchie," said Jinnet, "but I havena seen the colour o' his money yet."

"Study! study!" said Erchie. "Ye canna expect the puir lad to be thinkin' even-on aboot his lessons, and learnin' Latin and the rest o't, no' to mention 'Mush Mush,' and still keep mind o' your twa or three paltry bawbees."

"I mentioned it to him on Setturday and he was rale annoyed. He yoked on me and said I was jist as bad as the weedow he lodged wi' afore; that he was shair I was gaun to let the tear doon-fa'. He gied me warnin' that if I let the tear doon-fa' he wad leave."

"If I was you I wad start greetin' at yince," said Erchie. "And he'll leave onywye, this very Setturday."

That afternoon the students were having torchlight procession, when, as usual, most of them marched in masquerade. It was the day of the Rectorial Election, and the dust of far-flung pease-meal—favourite missile of the student—filled the air all over the classic slopes of Gilmorehill. It had been one of Erchie's idle days. He had been in the house all afternoon, and still was unbedded, though Jinnet for once had retired without waiting the home-coming of her lodger.

There came a riotous singing of students along the street, accompanied by the wheezy strains of a barrel-organ, and for twenty minutes uproar reigned at the entrance to the MacPherson's close.

Then Tod came up and opened the door with his latch-key. He had on part of Erchie's professional habiliments—the waiter's dress-coat and also Erchie's Sunday silk hat, both surreptitiously taken from a press in the lobby. They were foul with pease-meal and the melted rosin from torches. On his shoulders Tod had strapped a barrel-organ, and the noise of it, as it thumped against the door-posts on his entry, brought Erchie out to see what was the matter.

He took in the situation at a glance, though at first he did not recognise his own clothes.

"It's you. Mr Tod!" said he. "I was jist sittin' here thinkin' on ye slavin' awa' at your lessons yonder in the Deveenity Hall. It maun be an awfu' strain on the intelleck. I'm gled I never went to the college mysel', but jist got my education, as it were, by word o' mooth."

Tod breathed heavily. He looked very foolish with his borrowed and begrimed clothes, and the organ on his back, and he realised the fact himself.

"'S all ri', Mr MacPherson," he said. "Music hath charms. Not a word! I found this—this instuiment outside, and just took it home. Thought it might be useful. Music in the house makes cheerful happy homes—see advertisements—so I borrowed this from old friend, what's name—Angina Pectoris, Italian virtuoso, leaving him the monkey. Listen."

He unslung the organ and was starting to play it in the lobby when Erchie caught him by the arm and restrained him.

"Canny, man, canny," said he. "Did I no' think it was a box wi' your bursary. I never kent richt whit a bursary was, but the lad o' pairts in the novells aye comes hame wi' a bursary, and hurts the spine o' his back carryin' his prizes frae the college. I jalouse that's the hectic flush on your face. Puir laddie, ye're no' lang for this warld."

Erchie stared more closely at his lodger, and for the first time recognised his own swallow-tail coat.

"My goodness!" said he, "my business coat, and my beadlin' hat. It was rale ill done o' ye, Mr Tod, to tak' them oot withoot my leave. It's the first time ever I was ashamed o' them. Jist a puir auld waiter's coat and hat. I wonder whit they wad say if they kent o't up in Clachnacudden. The auld dominie that was sae prood o' ye wad be black affronted. My business coat! Tak' it aff and gang to your bed like a wise man. Leave the hurdy-gurdy on the stair-heid. Ye divna ken whit the other monkey micht hae left aboot it, and Jinnet's awfu' parteecular."

★　　　★　　　★

Next day Mr Tod got a week's notice to remove, and went reluctantly, for he knew good lodgings when he got them. He paid his bill when he went, too 'like a gentleman,' as Jinnet put it. "He was a rale cheery wee chap," she said.

"I've seen faur worse," Erchie admitted. "Foolish a wee, but Nature, the Rale Oreeginal! I was gey throughither mysel' when I was his age. Ye never tellt me yet whit ye wanted wi' the ludging money."

I was jist thinkin' I wad like to see ye wi' a gold watch the same as Carmichael's, next door," said Jinnet. "It's a thing a man at your time o' life, and in your poseetion, should hae, and I was ettlin' to gie ye't for your New Year."

"A gold watch!" cried her husband. "Whit nonsense!"

"It's no' nonsense at a'," said Jinnet. "It gies a man a kind o' bien, weel-daein' look, and I thocht I could mak' enough aff ludgers to buy ye yin."

"If it was for that ye wanted the ludger, and no' for a motor cairrage," said Erchie, "I'm gled Tod's awa'. You and your watch! I wad be a bonny like la-di-da wi' a watch at the waitin'. The folks wad be feared to tip me in case I wad be angry wi' them."

And so Erchie has not yet got a gold watch.

XVI

JINNET'S TEA-PARTY

Erchie's goodwife came to him one day full of thrilling news from the dairy, where she had been for twopence worth of sticks.

"Oh, Erchie, dae ye ken the latest?" said she. "The big fat yin in the dairy's gaun to mairry Duffy!"

"Lord peety Duffy! Somebody should tell the puir sowl she has her e'e on him. I'll bate ye he disna ken anything aboot it," said Erchie.

"Havers!" said Jinnet. "It's him that's wantin' her, and I'm shair it's a guid thing, for his hoose is a' gaun to wreck and ruin since his last wife dee'd. Every time he comes hame to dry his claes on a wet day he's doon in the dairy for anither bawbee's worth o' mulk. The man's fair hoved up wi' drinkin' mulk he's no needin'. I hae catched him there that aften that he's kind o' affronted to see me. 'I'm here again, Mrs MacPherson,' says he to me yesterday when I went doon and found him leanin' ower the coonter wi' a tumbler in his haund. He was that ta'en he nearly dropped the gless."

"It wasna for the want o' practice—I'll wager ye that!" said Erchie. "He could haud a schooner a hale nicht and him hauf sleepin'."

'I'm here again,' says he, onywye; 'the doctor tellt me yon time I had the illness I was to keep up my strength. There's a lot o' nourishment in mulk.' and the big yin's face was as red as her shortgoon.

'It's a blessin' the health, Mr Duffy,' says I, 'we divna ken whit a mercy it is till we lose it,' and I never said anither word, but took my bit sticks and cam' awa'.'

"And is that a' ye hae to gang on to be blamin' the chap?" said Erchie' "Mony's a man 'll tak' a gless o' mulk and no' go ower faur wi't. But I think mysel' ye're maybe richt aboot the big yin, for I see Duffy's shaved aff his Paisley whiskers, and wears a tie on the Sundays."

Less than a week later the girl in the dairy gave in her notice, and Duffy put up the price of coals another ha'penny. He came up the stairs with two bags for Jinnet, who was one of his customers.

"Whit wye are they up a bawbee the day?" says she.

"It's because o' the Americans dumpin'," said Duffy. "They're takin' a' the tred frae us, and there's a kind o' tariff war."

"Bless me! Is there anither war?" said Jinnet. "Weel, they're gettin' a fine day for't onywye. I hope it'll no put up the price o' the

71

mulk."

Duffy looked at her and laughed uneasily. "I'm kind o' aff the mulk diet the noo," said he, seeing disguise was useless. "Ye're gey gleg, you weemen. I needna be tellin' ye me and big Leezie's sort o' chief this while back."

"Man! dae ye tell me?" said Jinnet, innocently. "A rale dacent lassie, and bakes a bonny scone. And she's to be the new mistress, is she? "We'll hae to be savin' up for the jeely-pan. I'm shair I aye tellt Erchie a wife was sair wanted in your hoose since Maggie dee'd."

"Jist at the very time I was thrangest," said Duffy, with regret. "I was awfu' chawed at her."

"Ye'll hae to bring yer lass up to see me and Erchie some nicht," said Jinnet. "It's a tryin' time the mairryin'."

"There faur ower mony palavers aboot it," confided the coalman. "I wish it was ower and done wi', and I could get wearin' my grauvit at nicht again. Leezie's awfu' pernicketty aboot me haein' on a collar when we gang for a walk."

"Oh, ye rascal!" said Jinnet, roguishly. "You men! you men! Ah, the coortin' time's the best time."

"Ach! it's richt enough, I daursay, but there's a lot o' nonsense aboot it. Ye get awfu' cauld feet standin' in the close. And it's aye in yer mind. I went to Leezie's closemooth the ither nicht to whistle on her, and did I no' forget, and cry oot 'Coal!' thinkin' I was on business."

And thus it was that Jinnet's tea-party came about. The tender pair of pigeons were the guests of honour, and Jinnet's niece, and Macrae the night policeman, were likewise invited. Macrae was there because Jinnet thought her niece at thrityfive was old enough to marry. Jinnet did not know that he had drunk milk in Leezie's dairy before Duffy had gone there, and he himself had come quite unsuspicious of whom he should meet. In all innocence Jinnet had brought together the elements of tragedy.

There was something cold in the atmosphere of the party, Erchie noticed it. "Ye wad think it was a Quakers' meetin'," he said to himself, as all his wife's efforts to encourage an airy conversation dismally failed.

"See and mak' yer tea o't, Mr Macrae," she said to the night policeman. "And you, Sarah, I wish ye would tak' yin o' thae penny things, and pass the plate to Mr Duffy. Ye'll excuse there bein' nae scones, Mr Duffy, there hasna been a nice scone baked in the dairy since Leezie left. There's wan thing ye'll can be shair o' haein' when ye're mairret to her, and that's guid bakin'."

Macrae snorted.

"What's the maitter wi' dough-feet, I wonder?". thought Erchie, as innocent as his wife was of any complication. "That's the worst o' askin' the polis to yer pairties—they're no cless, and I'm shair, wi' a' Jinnet's contrivance, Sarah wadna be made up wi' him."

"A wee tate mair tea, Mr Macrae? Leezie, gie me Mr Macrae's cup if it's oot."

Macrae snorted again. "I'll not pe puttin' her to the bother, Mrs MacPherson," said he, "Murdo Macrae can be passin' his own teacups without botherin' anybody."

"Dough-feet's in the dods," thought Erchie, to whom the whole situation was now, for the first time, revealed like a flash.

"I think, Jinnet," said he, "ye wad hae been nane the waur o' a pun' or twa o' conversation-losengers."

They ate oranges after tea, but still a depression hung upon the company like a cloud, till Erchie asked Macrae if he would sing.

"Onything ye like," said he, "as lang's it's no' yin o' yer tartan chats that has a hundred verses, and that needs ye to tramp time wi' yer feet till't. I've a flet fit mysel', though my hert's warm, and I'm nae use at batin' time."

Macrae looked at Leezie, who had all night studiously evaded his eye, cleared his throat, and started to sing a song with the chorus—

"Fause Maggie Jurdan,
She made my life a burden;
I don't want to live,
And I'm gey sweart to dee.
She's left me a' forlorn,
And I wish I'd ne'er been born,
Since fause Maggie Jurdan
Went and jilted me."

Leezie only heard one verse, and then began hysterically to cry.

"Look you here, Mac," broke in Erchie, "could ye no' mak' it the sword dance, or the Hoolichan, or something that wadna harrow oor feelin's this way?"

"Onything that'll gie us a rest," said Duffy, soothing he fiancée. "The nicht air's evidently no' very guid for the voice."

"Coals!" cried the policeman, in a very good imitation of Duffy's business wail and, at that, Leezie had to be assisted into the kitchen by the other two women.

Duffy glared at his jealous and defeated rival, thought hard of something withering to hurl at him, and then said "Saps!"

"What iss that you are saying?" asked Macrae.

"Saps! Big Saps! That's jist what ye are," said Duffy. "If I wasna engaged I wad gie ye yin in the ear."

Jinnet's tea-party broke up as quickly as possible after that. When her guests had gone, and she found herself alone in the kitchen with Erchie and the tea dishes he carried in for her, she fell into a chair and wept.

"I'll never hae anither tea-pairty, and that's tellin' ye," she exclaimed between her sobs. "Fancy a' that cairry-on ower a big, fat, cat-witted cratur like thon! Her and her lads!"

"It's a' richt, Jinnet," said Erchie; "you syne oot the dishes and I'll dry them if ye'll feenish yer greetin'. It's no' the last tea-pairty we'll hae if we hae oor health, but the next yin ye hae see and pick the company better."

XVII

THE NATIVES OF CLACHNACUDDEN

"You are looking somewhat tired Erchie," I said to the old man on Saturday. "I suppose you were waiter at some dinner last night?"

"Not me!" said he promptly. "I wasna at my tred at a' last nicht, I was wi' Jinnet at the Clachnacudden conversashion. My! but we're gettin' grand. You should hae seen the twa o' us sittin' as hard as onything in a corner o' the hall watchin' the young yins dancin', and wishin' we were hame. Och, it's a fine thing a conversashion. There's naething wrang wi't. It's better than standin' aboot the street corners, or haudin' up the coonter at the Mull o' Kintyre Vaults. But I'll tell ye whit, it's no' much o' a game for an auld couple weel ower sixty, though no' compleenin', and haein' their health, and able to read the smallest type withoot specs. I wadna hae been there at a', but Macrae, the nicht polisman that's efter Jinnet's niece, cam' cravin' me to buy tickets."

'I'm no' a Clachnacudden native,' says I to him. 'If it was a reunion o' the natives o' Gorbals and district, it micht be a' richt, for that's the place I belang to. And if a' the auld natives cam' to a Gorbals swaree I micht get some o' the money some o' them's owin' me. But Clachnacudden!—I never saw the place, I aye thocht it was jist yin o' thae comic names they put on the labels o' the whisky bottles to mak' the look fancy.'

"Ye'll no' believe't, but Macrae, bein' Hielan' and no' haein' richt English, was that angry for me sayin' that aboot Clachnacudden, that he was nearly breakin' the engagement wi' Jinnet's niece, and I had to tak' the tickets at the hinnerend jist for peace' sake. Jinnet said it was a bonny-like thing spilin' Sarah's chances for the sake o' a shillin' or twa.

"So that's the wye I was wi' the Clachnacudden chats. Dae ye no' feel the smell o' peat-reek aff me? If it wasna that my feet were flet I could gie ye the Hielan' Fling.

"But thae natives' reunions in Gleska's no' whit they used to be. They're gettin' far ower genteel. It'll soon be comin' to't that ye'll no can gang to ony o' them unless ye have a gold watch and chain, a dress suit, and £10 in the Savin's Bank. It used to be in the auld days when I went to natives' gatherin's for fun, and no' to please the nicht polis, that they were ca'd a swaree and ball, and the ticket was four-and-six for yoursel' and your pairtner. If ye didna get the worth o' your money there was something wrang wi' your stomach, or ye werena very smert. Mony a yin I've bin at, either in the wye o' tred, or because some o' Jinnet's Hielan' kizzens cam' up to the hoose in their kilts to sell us tickets. There was nae dress suits nor fal-lals aboot a reunion in thae days. Ye jist put on your Sunday claes and some scent on your hanky, wi' a dram in your pocket (if ye werena in the committee), turned up the feet o' your breeks, and walked doon to the hall in the extra-wide welt shoes ye were gaun to dance in. Your lass—or your wife, if it was your wife—sat up the nicht before, washin' her white shawl and sewin' frillin' on the neck o' her guid frock, and a' the expense ye had wi' her if ye werena married to her was that ye had to buy her a pair o' white shammy leather gloves, size seeven.

"A' the auld folk frae Clachnacudden in Gleska were at thae swarees, as weel as a' the young folk. Ye were packed in your sates like red herrin' in a barrel, and on every hand ye heard folk tearin' the tartan and misca'in' somebody at hame in Clachnacudden. The natives wi' the dress suits that had got on awfu' weel in Gleska at the speerit tred or keeping banks, sat as dour as onything on the pletform lettin' on they couldna speak the tartan. Ithers o' them— that had the richt kind o' legs for't—wad hae on the kilts, wi' a white goat-skin sporran the size o' a door-bass hung doon to their knees, haudin' in their breaths in case the minister wad smell drink aff them, and tryin' to feel like Rob Roy or Roderick Dhu.

"In thae days they started oot wi' giein' ye tea and a poke o' fancy breid—penny things like London buns and fruitcakes and, between the speeches, oranges were passed roond and wee roond hard sweeties, fine for pappin' at the folk in front. Ye aye made a guid tea o't, the same as if ye never saw tea in your life afore, and preferred it weel biled.

"When the tea was bye and the boys were blawin' as much breath as they had left into the empty pokes, and bangin' them aff like cannons, the chairman wad stand up on the pletform and make a speech aboot Clachnacudden. I used to ken that speech by hert; it was the same yin for a' the natives' reunions. He said the Clachnacudden was the bonniest place ever onybody clapped eyes on. That the Clachnacudden men were notorious a' ower the wold for their honesty and push, and aye got on like onything if they were tryin', and didna tak' to the drink, and that the Clachnacudden lassies were that braw, and nice, and smert, they were lookit up to every place they went. When he said that the natives o' Clachnacudden kent fine it was the God's truth he was tellin' them, they got on their feet and waved their hankies and cheered for ten meenutes.

"Havin' taken a drink o' watter frae the caraffe at his side—efter makin' a mistake and tryin' to blaw the froth aff the tumbler—the chairman then begood generally to say that Gleska was a gey cauld, sooty, dirty, wicked place for onybody to hae to live in that had been born in the bonny wee glens, and the hulls, and hedges, and things aboot Clachnacudden, but still

'Their herts were true, their herts were Hielan',
And they in dreams beheld the Hebrides.'

At that ye wad see the hale o' the Clachnacudden folk puttin' whit was left o' their pastry in their pouches and haudin' their hankies wi' baith hands to their e'en to keep the tears frae rinnin' on their guid waistcoats or their silk weddin' goons. And the droll thing was that for a' they misca'd Gleska, and grat aboot Clachnacudden, ye couldna get yin o' them to gang back to Clachnacudden if ye pyed the train ticket and guaranteed a pension o' a pound a week.

"Clachnacudden bein' Hielan', they aye started the music efter the chairman's speech wi' a sang frae Harry Linn ca'd 'Jock Macraw, the Fattest Man in the Forty-Twa,' or some ither sang that kind o' codded themsel's. Then the minister made a comic speech wi' jokes in't, and tried to look as game as onything. And the folk frae Clachnacudden leaned forrit on their sates and asked the wifes in front if they had mind when his mither used to work in the tawtie field. 'Fancy him a minister!' says they, 'and tryin' to be comic, wi' his mither jist yin o' the MacTaggarts!' A' the time the puir minister was thinkin' he was daein' fine, and wonderin' if 'The Oban Times' was takin' doon a' his speech.

"And then a lot o' nyafs in the back sates aye began to heave orange-peelin's at folk that was daein' them nae hairm.

"Efter the swaree was ower, the weemen went into the ladies' room to tak' aff their galoshes, and tak' the preens oot o' their trains, and the men went ower to the Duke o' Wellington Bar, rinnin' like onything, for it was nearly eleeven o'clock. The folk the hall belanged to started to tak' oot the sates for the dancin', and sweep the corks aff the floor, and at eleeven prompt, the Grand Merch started. Whiles they had Adams' or Iff's band, and whiles they jist had Fitzgerald, the fiddler used to play on the Lochgoilhead boat. It didna maitter, for a' the Clachnacudden folk were fine strong dancers, and could dance to onything. Man! I aye liked the Grand Merch. The men wi' the reddest kilts aye started it at the Clachnacudden, and when the Grand Merch got a' fankled, they jist started 'Triumph,' and did the best they could.

"That was in the grand auld days afore they got genteel. Nooadays, as I'm tellin' ye, it's a' conversashions, and they work aff their speeches on ye wi' no tea at a' and no pokes o' pastry, nor naething. Ye're no use unless ye hae the lend o' a dress suit, and your pairtner has to hae pipe-clyed shoon, a muslin frock no' richt hooked at the neck, her hair put up at Bamber's, and a cab to tak' her hame in. It's naething but the waltzin'. I'm prood to say I never waltzed in a' my days, though they say I have the richt kind o' feet for't, me bein' so lang at the waitin'. And a' they auld classic dances, like La-va and the Guaracha Waltz and Circassian Circle's oot o' date. I havena even seen Petronella for mony a day.

"And the music's a' spiled. It's a' fancy music they hae noo, wi' nae tune ye can sing to't as ye gang up the back or doon the middle. Ye'll see them yonder wi' their piano, three fiddles, and a cornet. If I was gaun to hae a cornet I wad hae a cornet and no' a brass feenisher.

"Ye'll no' see ony o' the daecent auld Clachnacudden folk at their modern reunions. The puir sowls have to bide at hame and gang to their beds early that they may get up in time to mak' a cup o' tea for their dochters that was at the conversashion. No, Jinnet and me's no' keen on Clachnacudden or onything o' the kind nooadays. We wad faur sooner stay at hame and read 'The Weekly Mail.'"

XVIII

MARY ANN

"I see frae 'The News,'" said Erchie, "that Mary Ann's no' gaun to see her kizzen on her nicht oot the noo, but has the kitchen table cleared for action wi' a penny bottle o' Perth ink and a quire o' paper to write letters to the editor, telling him and his readers that the country doesna ken her value.

"If ye're in the habit o' tryin' to keep a general, ye canna be shair but at this very meenute she's doon the stair, wi' her sleeves rowed up and her fingers a' Perth Blue Black, paintin' your wife's photograph as a slave-driver, and givin' your hoose a character that would mak' ye lose your nicht's sleep if ye kent it. Faith, it's comin' to it!

"The servant problem is the only ane that's railly o' ony interest to the country, as far as I can mak' oot frae hearin' things when I'm either beadlin', or waitin' at waddin'-breakfasts. Twa women canna put their heads thegither ower a cup o' tea withoot gaun ower a list o' a' the lassies they've had since last November, and the notion ye get is that they change frae place to place that often they must hae motor cairrages.

"Mary Ann sails in with her kist and a fine character frae her last place on Monday at 8p.m., and aboot ten minutes efter that she's on the road again. She is the greatest traveller o' the age. It is estimated by them that kens aboot thae things, that the average domestic, if she keeps her health and gets ony chance at a' gangs 15,000 miles every three years shifting her situation.

"It is the age of the lairge-build, agile, country girl. No ither kind can stand the strain o' humpin' kists up and doon those stairs. An aluminium kist that, when packed weighs only fifteen pounds, has been invented specially for the 'strong and willing general, early riser, no washin', fond o' weans'. But, in spite o' that, she canna get ower mair nor 250 to 263 different situations in the year.

"The Hielan's is the peculiar home o' the maist successful domestic servants, though a very gude strain o' them is said to come frae Ayrshire and roon' aboot Slamannan.

"They are catched young, carefully clipped, curry-combed and shod, and shipped to Gleska at the beginnin' o' the winter, wi' fine characters frae the U.F. minister. On the day they start their first situation they're generals, that say 'Whit is't?' quite angry, at the door to folk that come to their mistress's efternoon teas. On the Wednesday they're wanting their wages up, and on the Thursday they start in anither place as experienced 'hoose-and-table-maids'. At least, that's whit I gaither frae overhearin' the ladies. We have nae servant in oor hoose,—Jinnet does everything hersel'.

"When Mary Ann's no' packin' her kist, or haein' confabs wi' the butcher, or trimmin' a frock for the Clachnacudden natives' swarree and ball, she's lookin' the papers to see the rate o' servants' wages in Kimberley, near whaur the wars were. Some day she's gaun to Kimberley, or Australia, or ony ither foreign pairt, whaur intelligent cooks get the wages o' Cabinet Ministers, and can get mairrit jist as easy's onything.

"In the fine auld times servant lassies used to bide wi' ye till they were that auld and frail ye had to have somebody sittin' up wi' them at nicht.

"Yince they got a fit in yer hoose ye couldna get quat o' them. They fastened their kists to the floor wi' big screwnails, and wad scarcely go oot the length o' the kirk for fear ye wad shut up the hoose and rin awa' and leave them. As for the wages they got, they were that sma', folks used to toss up a bawbee to see whether they wad keep a servant or a canary.

"But nooadays a man that's in the habit o' payin' ony heed to the servant lassies that opens the door for him or hands him his letters, thinks it's a magic-lantern show he's at, wi' a new picture every twa seconds.

"He doesna see his wife except on the Sundays, for a' the ither days o' the week she's cyclin' roond the registries wi' five pounds o' change in silver, payin' fees."

'Hoose-tablemaid, ma'am? Certainly, ma'am; we'll see whit we can dae for ye between noo and the next Gleska Exhibeetion,' says the registry, rakin' in the half-croons as hard's she can.

"When there's a rumour gets aboot Dowanhill that a servant lass, oot o' a situation, was seen the week afore last, hundreds o' ladies mak' for the registries, and besiege them in the hope o' catchin' her, and of late, I'm tellt they're engagin' trained detectives for trackin' plain cooks.

"Domestic service is the only profession in Europe the day whaur the supply's less than the demand, and if I had twa or three boys ready to gang oot and work for themselves, I wad sooner mak' them into scullery-maids than apprentice them wi' an electrical engineer.

"In the last ten years wha ever heard o' a servant lassie oot o' a situation ony langer than the time she took to rin frae ae hoose to anither, if she had the richt number of hands and een?"

"She disna need to gang onywhere lookin' for a place; the sleuth-hounds o' Dowanhill track her to her lair as soon as she's landed at the Broomielaw or Buchanan Street Station, and mak' a grab at her afore she learns enough o' the language to ask her wye to a registry.

"A new servant in a hoose is like a Field-Marshal back frae the front. She's trated wi' sae muckle deference. Ye daurna mak' a noise through the day for fear it'll spoil her sleep. Ye pit on the fire for her in the mornin', and brush her golfin' buits afore ye start for the office. Ye pay sixpence a day o' car fares for her to go and see her kizzens in case she's wearyin', puir thing! And if 'Rob Roy's' on at the theatre ye'll be as weel to let her know and gie her tickets for it, or she'll gie notice when she reads the creeticism in the paper and finds oot she missed it. Mair than a dizzen societies have been started for giving medals and rewards to servant lassies that have been a lang, lang while in the ae situation; they're worked on a graduated scale:

– Hoosemaids, in one situation two months—Bronze medal of the Society and 30 shillings.

– Generals, three months—Silver medal and fountain pen.

– Plain cook, six months—Gold medal, £5, and gramophone.

"Whit the country wants is the municeepilistion o' domestic service. The better hoosin' o' the poor's a thing that there's nae hurry for. Plain cooks and general servants that ken the difference between a cake o' black lead and a scrubbin-brush are a communal needcessity. They can nae mair be done without than gas, water, skoosh cars, or the telephone.

"The Corporations should import and train Mary Anns in bulk, gie them a nate uniform and thirty shillin's a week, and hire them oot 'oorly, daily, weekly, or monthly, as required, reserving for them a' the rights and privileges that belong to them, wi' limitation o' working' 'oors, strick definition o' duties, stipulated nichts oot, and faceelities for followers. Look at the polis. Ye can depend on gettin' a polisman nine times oot o' ten if ye want him. A lassie to go oot wi' the pramlater, or a hoose-tablemaid, should be jist as easy got by every ratepayer when wanted, and that's only to be secured by the Corporations takin' the domestic service into their ain haunds."

XIX
DUFFY'S WEDDING

I did not see Erchie during the New Year holidays, and so our greetings on Saturday night, when I found him firing up the church furnace, had quite a festive cheerfulness.

"Where have you been for the past week?" I asked him. "It looks bad for a beadle to be conspicuous by his absence at this season of the year."

"If ye had been whaur ye ocht to hae been, and that was in the kirk last Sunday, ye wad hae found me at my place," said Erchie. "Here's a bit bride's-cake," he went on, taking a little packet from his pocket. "The rale stuff! Put that below your heid at nicht and ye'll dream aboot the yin that's gaun to mairry ye. It's a sure tip, for I've kent them that tried it, and escaped in time."

I took the wedding cake. To dream of the one I want to marry is the desire of my days though, indeed, I don't need any wedding-cake below my pillow for such a purpose. "And who's wedding does this—this deadly comestible—come from Erchie?" I asked him.

"Wha's wad it be but Duffy's," said Erchie. 'At 5896 Baird Street, on the 31st, by the Rev. J. Macauslane, Elizabeth McNiven Jardine to James K. Duffy, coal merchant.' Duffy's done for again. Ye'll can see him noo hurryin' hame for his tea when his work's bye and feared ony o' the regular customers o' the Mull of Kintyre Vaults will stop him on the road and ask him in for something. His wife's takin' him roond wi' a collar on, and showin' him aff among a' her freen's and the ither weemen she wants to vex, and she's learning him to ca' her "Mrs D.' when they're in company. He wasna twa days at his work efter the thing happened when she made him stop cryin' his ain coals and leave yin o' his men to dae't, though there's no' twa o' them put thegither has the voice o' Duffy. I wadna wonder if his tred fell aff on accoont o't, and it's tellin' on his health. 'She says it's no' genteel for me to be cryin' my ain coals,' he says to me; 'but I think it's jist pride on her part, jist pride. Whit hairm does it dae onybody for me to gie a wee bit roar noo and then if it's gaun to help business?' I heard him tryin' to sing 'Dark Lochnagar' on Friday nicht in his ain hoose, and it wad vex ye to listen, for when he was trampin' time wi' his feet ye could hardly hear his voice, it was that much failed. 'Duffy,' I says to him, takin' him aside, 'never you mind the mistress, but go up a close noo and then and gie a roar to keep your voice in trim withoot lettin' on to her onything aboot it.'

"Yes, Duffy was mairried on Hogmanay Nicht, and we were a' there, Jinnet and me and her niece Sarah, and Macrae the nicht polis, and a companion o' Macrae's frae Ardentinny that had his pipes wi' him to play on, but never got them tuned. It was a grand ploy, and the man frae Ardentinny fell among his pipes comin' doon the stair in the mornin'. 'Ye had faur ower much drink,' I tellt him, takin' him oot frae amang the drones and ribbons and things. 'I'm shair ye've drunk a hale bottle.'

'Whit's a bottle o' whusky among wan?' says he. If it wasna for him it wad hae been a rale nice, genteel mairrage.

"Duffy had on a surtoo coat, and looked for a' the warld like Macmillan, the undertaker, on a chape job. He got the lend o' the surtoo frae yin o' the men aboot the Zoo, and he was aye tryin' to put his haunds in the ootside pooches and them no' there. 'Oh, Erchie,' he says to me, 'I wish I had on my jaicket again, this is no canny. They'll a' be lookin' at my haunds.'

'No, nor yer feet,' I tellt him; 'they'll be ower busy keepin' their e'e on whit they're gaun to get to eat.'

'If ye only kent it,' says he, 'my feet's a torment to me, for by buits is far ower sma'.' And I could see the puir sowl sweatin' wi' the agony.

"The bride looked fine. Jinnet nearly grat when she saw her comin' in, and said it minded her o' hersel' the day she was mairried. 'Ye're just haverin',' I tellt her, gey snappy, 'She couldna look as nice as you did that day if she was hung wi' jewels.' But I'll no' say Leezie wasna nice enough, a fine big, sonsy, smert lass, wi' her face as glossy as onything.

"When the operation was by, and the minister had gane awa' hame, us pressin' him like onything to wait a while langer, and almost breakin' his airms wi' jammin' his top-coat on him fast in case he micht change his mind, we a' sat doon to a high tea that wad dae credit to F. & F.'s. If there was wan hen yonder there was haulf a dizzen, for the bride had a hale lot o' country freen's, and this is the time o' the year the hens is no' layin'.

"There were thirty-five folk sat doon in Duffy's hoose that nicht, no' coontin' a wheen o' the neighbours that stood in the lobby and took their chance o' whit was passin' frae the kitchen. Duffy hadna richt started carvin' the No.6 hen when a messenger cam' to the door to ask for the surtoo coat, because the man in the Zoo had his job changed for that nicht and found he needed the coat for his work. So Duffy was quite gled to get rid of it, and put on his Sunday jaicket. 'Ask him if he wadna like a wee lend o' my new tight boots,' he says to the messenger frae the Zoo, 'if he does, come back as fast's ye can for them, and I'll pay the cab.'

"Efter the high tea was by, the Ardentinny man never asked onybody's leave, but began to tune his pipes, stoppin' every twa or three meenutes to bounce aboot the player he was, and that his name was McKay—yin o' the auld clan McKays. Macrae, the nicht polis, was awfu' chawed that he brocht him there at a'. Ye couldna hear yersel' speakin' for the tunin' o' the pipes, and they werena nearly half ready for playin' on when the bride's mither took the liberty o' stoppin' him for a wee while till we wad get a sang frae somebody."

'James 'll sing,' says the bride, lookin' as prood's ye like at her new man. 'Will ye no' obleege the company wi' 'Dark Lochnagar'?'

'I wad be only too willin',' he tellt her, 'if I had on my ither boots and hadna ett thon last cookie.' But we got him to sing 'Dark Lochnagar' a' richt. In the middle o't the man frae Ardentinny said, if Duffy wad haud on a wee while he wad accompany him on the pipes, and he started to tune them again. But Macrae stopped him by puttin' corks in his drones.

"Jinnet sang the 'Auld Hoose.' Man! I was prood o' her. Yon's the smertest wumman in Gleska. The Rale Oreeginal!"

"Don't you yourself sing, Erchie?"

"Not me! I'm comic enough withoot that. A flet fit and a warm hert, but timmer in the tune. Forbye, I was too busy keepin' doon the man frae Ardentinny. He was determined to hae them pipes o' his tuned if it took him a' nicht. I tried to get him to gang oot into the back-coort to screw them up, but he aye said they were nearly ready noo, they wadna tak' him ten meenutes, and he kept screechin' awa' at them. It was fair reediculous.

"At last the bride's mither got him put into the kitchen, and was clearin' the room for a dance. Duffy was very red in the face, and refused to rise frae the table. 'Whit's the use o' dancin'?' says he; 'are we no' daein' fine the way we are?' And then it was found oot he had slipped his tight boots aff him under the table, and was sittin' there as joco as ye like in his stockin' soles.

"The young yins were dancin' in the room to the playin' o' a whustle, and the rest o' us were smokin' oot on the stairheid, when the man frae Ardentinny cam fleein' oot wi' his bagpipes still gaspin'.

He said it was an insult to him to start dancin' to a penny whustle and him there ready to play if he could only get his pipes tuned."

'Never you heed, Mac,' says I; 'ye'll hae a chance at Macrae's waddin' if ye can get the pipes tuned afore then. He's engaged to oor Sarah.'

"I was that gled when the cat-wutted cratur fell amang his pipes gaun doon the stair in the mornin'; it served him richt."

"And where did Duffy and his bride spend their honeymoon, Erchie?" I asked.

"They took the skoosh car oot to Paisley. That was a' their honeymoon."

XX

ON CORPORAL PUNISHMENT

"On this question of corporal punishment in the schools, Erchie," I said to my old friend, "what are your views?" I've no doubt you're dead against any alteration on use and wont."

"Whiles," said Erchie; "whiles! I buy the paper ae day, and when I read the wye brutal and ignorant schoolmaisters abuse their poseetion, I feel that angry I could fling bricks at the windows o' a' the schools I pass on the wye to my wark. But the next day when I read whit perfect wee deevils a' the weans is nooadays, and hoo they'll a' turn oot a disgrace to their faithers and mithers if they divna get beltin' twice a day, I'm sair tempted to gae ower to my guid-dochter's in the Calton and tak' a razor-strop to wee Alick afore he gangs to his bed, jist in case he's bein' negleckit. That's the warst o' the newspapers; they're aye giein' ye the different sets o't, and ye read sae much on the ae side and then the ither that ye're fair bate to mak' up your mind. My ain puir auld faither—peace be wi' him!— didna seem to be muckle fashed wi' the different sets o't in the newspapers. He made up his mind awfu' fast, and gied ye his fit-rule ower the back o' the fingers afore ye could gie your wee brither a clip on the nose for clypin' on ye. They may abolish corporal punishment in the Gleska schools, but they'll no' pit an end to't in hooses whaur the faither's a plumber and aye has a fit-rule stuck doon the outside seam o' his breeks."

"Ah yes! Erchie, but these paternal ebullitions of ill-temper——"

"Ill-temper or no'," said Erchie, "it's a' in the scheme o' nature, and an angry man's jist as much the weapon o' nature as a thunderbolt is, or a lichted caundle lookin' for an escape o' gas. If ye didna get your licks in the school for bein' late in the mornin', ye'll get fined an awfu' lot o' times for sleepin' in when ye're auld enough to work in Dubs's. So the thing's as braid as it's wide, as the Hielan'man said."

"Then you seem to think a fit of anger is essential to parental punishment, Erchie? That's surely contrary to all sober conclusions."

"Sober conclusions hae naethin' to dae wi' skelpin' weans, as I ken fine that brocht up ten o' a family and nearly a' that's spared o' them daein' weel for themsel's. The auld Doctor in oor kirk talks aboot love and chastisement, but in my experience human nature wad be a' to bleezes lang afore this if faithers and mithers didna whiles lose their tempers and gie their weans whit they deserved. If you're the kind o' man that could thrash a puir wee smout o' a laddie in cauld bluid, I'm no', and I canna help it."

"And did you thrash your ten much, Erchie?" I asked, with a doubt as to that essential ill-temper in his case.

"That has naethin' to dae wi't," said he, quickly. "My private disinclination to hae the wee smouts greetin' disna affect the point at a'. If oor yins needed it, I went oot for a daunder and left the job to Jinnet. A woman's aye the best hand at it, as I ken by my aunty Chirsty. When she had the threshin' o' me, she aye gied me tuppence efter it was done if I grat awfu' sair, and I took guid care I never went wantin' money in thae days. I was only vexed she couldna thresh me threepence-worth the time the shows were roond oor wye, and mony's the time I worked for't.

"When the papers mak' me wonder whether corporal punishment's guid for the young or no'. I jist tak' a look at mysel' in Jinnet's new wardrobe looking gless, and except for the fleet feet—me bein' a waiter—I don't see muckle wrang wi' Erchie MacPherson, and the Lord kens there was nae slackness o' corporal punishment in his days, though then it was simply ca'd a leatherin'. My mither threshed me because it wadna gae wrang onywye—if I wasna need'nt the noo I wad be need'nt some ither time. And my faither threshed me because there was a hard knot in the laces o' his boots, and he couldna' lowse't. It didna dae me ony hairm, because I ken't they were fond enough o' me.

"In the school we were weel threshed in the winter-time to keep us warm, and in the summer-time a stirrin'-up wi' the tawse a' roond made up for the want o' ventilation. If I never learned much else in the school, I got a fair grup o' naitural history, and yin o' the tips I got was that a horsehair laid across the loof o' the haund 'll split a cane or cut the fingers aff a tawse, when ye're struck by either the yin or the ither. I made twa or three cairt-horses bald-heided at the tail wi' my experimentin', but somethin' aye went wrang. The maister either let fly ower sudden, or it was the wrang kind o' horse—at onyrate, I never mind o' cuttin' the cane or the tawse.

"Whiles, when I'm across at my guid-dochter's, I hear her wee laddie, Alick, greetin' ower his coonts, and fear't the maister 'll cane him because they're no' richt."

'If a cistern wi' an inlet pipe twa-and-a-half inches in diameter lets in seventy-nine gallons eleeven quarts and seeven pints in twentyfower and a half 'oors, and an ootlet pipe o' three-quarters o' an inch diameter discharges forty-eight gallons nineteen quarts and five pints in six 'oors, whit o'clock will the cistern be empty if the ootlet pipe hiz a big leak in't?

"That's the kind o' staggerer puir wee Alick gets thrashed for if ye canna answer't richt. I couldna dae a coont like that mysel', as shair's death, if I was paid for't, unless I had the cistern aside me, and a len' o' the measures frae the Mull o' Kintyre Vaults, and Jinnet wi' a lump o' chalk keepin' tally. I'm no' shair that it's ony guid to thrash wee Alick for no' daein' a count o' that kind, or for no' bein' able to spell 'fuchsia,' or for no' mindin' the exact heights o' a' the principal mountains in Asia and Sooth America.

"Noo, wad ye like it yoursel'? Ye canna put mathematics into a callan's heid by thrashin' him ower the fingers. If he's no' made wi' the richt lump in his heid for mathematics, and if Alick's schoolmaister gaes on thinkin' he can, I'll gae oot some day to his school and maybe get the jyle for't."

"Come, come, Erchie," I protested; "you are in quite an inconsistent humour to-day. Surely Alick's thrashings are all in the scheme of nature. If he is not punished now for inability to do that interesting proposition in compound proportion, he will be swindled out of part of his just payment when paid for bricklaying by the piece when he has taken to the trade, and the thing—once more as the Highlandman said—is as broad as it's wide."

"Nane o' my guid-dochter's sons is gaun to tak' to treds," said Erchie, coldly; "they're a' gaun to be bankers and electreecians and clerks and genteel things o' that sort. If I'm no' consistent aboot this, it's because o' whit I tellt ye, that I've read ower mony o' thae letters and interviews in the papers, and canna mak' up my mind. I ken fine a' the beltin's I got in the school were for my guid, but—but—but it's different wi' wee Alick."

"But we all have our wee Alicks, Erchie."

"Then we're a' weel aff," said Erchie, glowing, "for yon's the comicalest wee trate! The Rale Oreeginal."

"But the teachers don't understand him?"

"That's the hale p'int," said Erchie, agreeably, "the teachers never dae. They're no' paid for understandin' a' the wee Alick's. A' that can be expected for the wages the schoolmaisters get in Gleska is that they'll haul the wee cratur by the scruff o' the neck through a' the standards. The schoolmaister and the mither ought to be mair prized and bigger paid than ony ither cless in the country, but they're no', and that's the reason their jobs are often sae badly filled up.

"If education was a' that folk think it is, there wad lang syne hae been nae need for cane nor strap. For mair than a generation noo, every bairn has had to go to school—a' the parents o' a' the weans in school the noo have had an education themsel's, so that baith at hame, and in the school, the young generation of the present day have sae mony advantages ower whit you and I had, they ought to be regular gems o' guid behaviour and intelligence.

"But I canna see that they're ony better than their grand-faithers were at the same age. Except my guid-dochter's boy Alick, I think they're a' worse.

"A' the difference seems to be that they're auld sooner than we were, smoke sooner, and swear sooner, and in a hunner wyes need mair leatherin' than we did. Education o' the heid's no' education o' the hert, and the only thing that comes frae crammin' a callant o' naiturally bad disposeetion with book-learnin' is that he's the better trained for swindlin' his fellow-men when he's auld enough to try his hand at it. It wad be awfu' prood o' every new school that's in Gleska if I didna ken that I had to pay a polis tax for't by-and-bye as weel as school tax."

"How glad we ought to be, Erchie, that we were born in a more virtuous age," I said, and Erchie screwed up his face.

"We werena," said he. "It's aye been the same since the start o' things. I've jist been sayin' to ye whit I mind o' hearin' my faither say to mysel'. There'll aye be jist enough rogues in the world to keep guid folk like you and me frae gettin' awfu' sick o' each ither."

XXI

THE FOLLIES OF FASHION

My old friend has a great repugnance to donning new clothes. His wife, Jinnet, told me once she had always to let him get into a new suit, as it were, on the instalment system. The first Sunday he reluctantly put on the trousers. The second he ventured the trousers and waistcoat, and on the third he courageously went forth in the garb complete, after looking out at the close-mouth first to see that Duffy or any other ribald and critical acquaintance was not looking.

I saw a tell-tale crease down the front of the old man's legs yesterday.

"New sartorial splendour, Erchie?" I said, and pinched him for luck.

He got very red.

"You're awfu' gleg in the een." said he, "am I no' daein' my best to let on they're an auld pair cleaned? blame the wife for't! there's naethin' o' the la-di-da aboot easy-gaun Erchie. But weemen! claes is their hale concern since the day that Adam's wife got the shape o' a sark frae the deevil, and made it wi' a remender o' fig-leafs.

"There's no much wrang wi' Jinnet, but she's far ower pernicketty aboot whit her and me puts on, and if she has naething else to brag aboot she'll brag I hae aye the best brushed buits in oor kirk. She took an awfu' thraw yince at yin o' the elders, for she thocht he bate me wi' the polish o' his buits, and she could hardly sleep ower the heid o't till I tellt her they were patent."

'Och!' says she, 'is that a'? Patent's no' in the game.'

'Onything's in the game,' says I to her, 'that's chaper than heeling and soling.'

"It's bad enough," he went on, "to be hurtin' yer knees wi' new breeks, and haein' the folk lookin' at ye, but it's a mercy for you and me we're no weemen. You and me buys a hat, and as lang's the rim and the rest o't stick thegither, it's no' that faur oot the fashion we need to hide oorsel's. The only thing I see changes in is collars, and whether it's the lying-doon kind or the double-breisted chats, they hack yer neck like onything. There's changes in ties, but gie me plain black.

"Noo, Jinnet has to hae the shape o' her hat-shifted every month as regular's a penny diary. If it's flet in June, it's cockin' up in July, and if the bash is on the left side in August, it has to be on the right side in September.

"Och! but there's no muckle wrang wi' Jinnet for a' that. She wanted to buy me a gold watch-chain last Fair."

'A gold watch-chain's a nice, snod, bien-lookin' thing aboot a man,' she says, 'and it's gey useful.'

'No, nor useful,' says I, 'a watch-chain looks fine on a man, but it's his gallowses dae the serious wark.'

"Still, Erchie," I said, "oor sex can't escape criticism for its eccentricities of costume either. Just fancy our pockets, for instance?"

"Ye're right, there," Erchie agreed; "hae I no' fifteen pouches mysel' when I had my top-coat on? If I put a tramway ticket into yin o' them I wadna be able to fin' oot which o' them it was in for an 'oor or twa.

"Pockets is a rale divert. Ye canna dae withoot nine or ten in Gleska if ye try yer best. In the country it's different. Doon aboot Yoker, and Gargunnock, and Deid Slow and them places, a' man needs in the wye o' pouches is twa trooser yins—yin for each haund when he's leanin' against a byre-door wonderin' whit job he'll start the morn.

"There's a lot o' fancy wee pouches that'll no' haud mair than a pawn-ticket aboot a Gleska man's claes, but in the country they dae wi' less and dig them deep.

"Sae faur as I can see, the pouch is a new-fashioned thing a'thegither. Look at them auld chaps ye see in pictures wi' the galvanised or black-leaded suits on. If yin o' them wanted a pouch he wad need to cut it himsel' wi' a sardine-opener, and then he wad peel a' his knuckles feelin' for his hanky or the price o' a pint. I'm gled I wisna gaun aboot when them galvanised suits was the go. It must hae been awfu' sair on the nails scratchin' yersel'. Yer claes were made then in a biler-works. When ye went for the fit-on, the cutter bashed in the slack bits at the back wi' a hammer and made it easier for ye under the oxter wi' a cauld chisel."

'I want it higher at the neck,' says you.

'Right!' says he, quite game, and bangs in twa or three extra rivets. And your wife, if ye had yin, had to gie your suits a polish up every Friday when she was daein' the kitchen grate.

"It was the same when the Hielan's was the wye ye read aboot in books, and every Hielan'man wore the kilts.

"There was nae pockets in a pair of kilts.

"I daursay that was because the Hielan'man never had onything worth while to put in a pocket if he had yin. He hung his snuff-mull and his knife and fork ootside his claes, and kept his skean-dhu in his stockin'.

"It's a' proof that weemen's no' richt ceevilised yet that they can be daein', like the men I'm speaking aboot, withoot ony pooches. Jinnet tells me there's nae pooch in a woman's frock nooadays, because it wad spoil her sate on the bicycle. That's the wye ye see weemen gaun aboot wi' their purses in their haunds, and their bawbees for the skoosh car inside their glove, and their bonny wee watches that never gang because they're never rowed up, hingin' just ony place they'll hook on to ootside their claes.

"I was yince gaun doon to Whiteinch on a Clutha to see a kizzen o' the wife's, and Jinnet was wi' me. Me bein' caury-haunded, I got aff by mistake at Govan on the wrang side o' the river, when Jinnet was crackin' awa' like a pengun wi' some auld wife at the sherp end o' the boat, and she didna see me."

'Oh! Erchie!' she says when she cam' hame, 'the time I've put in! I thocht ye wis drooned.'

'And ye hurried hame for the Prudential book, I suppose?' says I.

'No,' says she, 'but I made up my mind to hae a pooch o' my ain after this, if I merrit again, to haud my ain Clutha fares, and no' be lippenin' to onybody.'"

92

XXII

ERCHIE IN AN ART TEA-ROOM

"I saw you and Duffy looking wonderfully smart in Sauchiehall Street on Saturday," I said to Erchie one morning.

"Man, were we no'?" replied the old man, with an amused countenance. "I must tell ye the pant we had. Ye'll no' guess where I had Duffy. Him and me was in thon new tea-room wi' the comic windows. Yin o' his horses dee'd on him, and he was doon the toon liftin' the insurance for't. I met him comin' hame wi' his Sunday claes on, and the three pound ten he got for the horse. He was that prood he was walkin' sae for back on his heels that a waff o' win' wad hae couped him, and whustlin' 'Dark Lochnagar.'"

'Come on in somewhere and hae something,' says he, quite joco.

'Not me,' says I—'I'm nane o' the kind. A beadle's a public man, and he disna ken wha may be lookin' at him, but I'll tell ye whit I'll dae wi' ye—I'll tak' ye into a tea-room.'

'A' richt,' says Duffy, 'I'm game for a pie or onything.'

"And I took him like a lamb to the new place."

"When we came fornent it, he glowered, and 'Michty!' says he, 'wha did this?'

'Miss Cranston,' says I.

'Was she tryin'?' says Duffy.

'She took baith hands to't,' I tellt him. 'And a gey smert wumman, too, if ye ask me.'

"He stood five meenutes afore I could get him in, wi' his een glued on the fancy doors."

'Do ye hae to break yer wey in?' says he.

'No, nor in,' I tells him, 'look slippy in case some o' yer customers sees ye!'

'Och! I havena claes for a place o' the kind,' says he, and his face red.

'Man!' I says, 'ye've henned—that's whit's wrang wi' ye. Come in jist for the pant. Naebody 'll touch ye, and ye'll can come oot if it's sore.'

"In we goes, Duffy wi' his kep aff. He gave the wan look roond him, and put his hand in his pooch to feel his money. 'Mind I have only the three flaffers and a half, Erchie,' says he.

'It'll cost ye nae mair than the Mull o' Kintyre Vaults,' I tellt him, and we began sclimmin' the stairs. Between every rail there was a piece o' gless like the bottom o' a soda-water bottle, hangin' on a wire, Duffy touched every yin o' them for luck.

'Whit dae ye think o' that, noo?' I asked him.

'It's gey fancy,' says Duffy; 'will we be lang?'

'Ye puir ignorant cratur!' I says, losin' my patience a'thegither, 'ye havena a mind in the dietin' line above a sate on the trams o' a lorry wi' a can o' soup in your hand.'

"I may tell ye I was a wee bit put aboot mysel', though I'm a waiter by tred, and seen mony a dydo in my time. There was naething in the hale place was the way I was accustomed to; the very snecks o' the doors were kind o' contrairy."

'This way for the threepeny cups and the guid bargains,' says I to Duffy, and I lands him into whit they ca' the Room de Looks. Maybe ye havena seen the Room de Looks; it's the colour o' a goon Jinnet used to hae afore we mairried. There's whit Jinnet ca's 'insertion' on the table-cloths, and wee beeds stitched a' ower the wa's, the same as if somebody had done it themsel's. The chairs is no' like ony ither chairs ever I clapped eyes on, but ye could easy guess they were chairs, and a' roond the place there's a lump o' lookin'-gless wi' purple leeks pented on it every noo and then. The gasalier in the middle was the thing that stunned me. It's hung a' roond wi' hunners o' big gless bools, the size o' yer nief—but ye don't get pappin' onything at them.

"Duffy could only speak in whispers. 'My jove!' says he, 'ye'll no' get smokin' here, I'll bate.'

'Smokin'!' says I; 'ye micht as weel talk o' gowfin'.'

'I never in a' my life saw the like o't afore. This cows a'!' says he, quite nervous and frichtened lookin'.

'Och!' says I, 'it's no' your fault, you didna dae't ony-wye. Sit doon.'

"There was a wheen lassies wi' white frocks and tippets on for waitresses, and every yin o' them wi' a string o' big red beads roond her neck."

'Ye'll notice, Duffy,' says I, 'that though ye canna get ony drink here, ye can tak' a fine bead onywye,' but he didna see my joke.

'Chaps me no'!' says he. 'Whit did ye say the name o' this room was?'

'The Room de Looks,' I tellt him.

'It'll likely be the Room de Good Looks,' says he, lookin' at the waitress that cam' for oor order. 'I'm for a pie and a bottle o' Broon

Robin.'

'Ye'll get naething o' the kind. Ye'll jist tak' tea, and stretch yer hand like a Christian for ony pastry ye want,' said I, and Duffy did it like a lamb. Oh! I had the better o' him. The puir sowl never saw onything fancy in his life afore since the time Glenroy's was shut in the New City Road, where the Zoo is. It was a rale divert. It was the first time ever he had a knife and fork to eat cookies wi', and he thocht his teaspoon was a' bashed oot o' its richt shape till I tellt him that was whit made it Art.

'Art,' says he, 'whit the mischief's Art?'

'I can easy tell ye whit Art is,' says I, 'for it cost me mony a penny. When I got mairried, Duffy, haircloth chairs was a' the go, the sofas had twa ends to them, and you had to hae six books wi' different coloured batters spread oot on the paurlor table, wi' the tap o' yer weddin'-cake under a gless globe in the middle. Wally dugs on the mantel-piece, worsted things on the chairbacks, a picture o' John Knox ower the kist o' drawers, and 'Heaven Help Our Home' under the kitchen clock. That was whit Jinnet and me started wi'. There's mony a man in Gleska the day buyin' hand-done pictures and wearin' tile hats to their work that begun jist like that. When Art broke oot——'

'I never took it yet,' says Duffy.

'I ken that,' says I, 'but it's ragin' a' ower the place. Ye'll be a lucky man if ye're no' smit wi't cairryin' coals up thae new tenements they ca' mansions, for that's a hotbed o' Art. But, as I say, when Art broke oot, Jinnet took it bad, though she didna ken the name o' the trouble, and the hair-cloth chairs had to go, and leather yins got, and the sofa wi' the twa ends had to be swapped for yin wi' an end cut aff and no' richt back. The wally dugs, and the worsted things, and the picture o' John Knox, were nae langer whit Jinnet ca'd the fashion, and something else had to tak' their place. That was Art. It's a lingerin' disease. She has the dregs o't yet, and whiles buys shillin' things that's nae use for onything except for dustin'.'

'Oh! is that it?' says Duffy, 'I wish I had a pie.'

'Ye'll get a pie then,' I tellt him, 'but ye canna expect it here. A pie's no becomin' enough for the Room de Looks. Them's no' chairs for a coalman to sit on eatin' pies.'

"We went doon the stair then, and I edged him into the solid meat department. There was a lassie sittin' at a desk wi' a wheen o' different coloured bools afore her, and when the waitresses cam' to he for an order for haricot mutton or roast beef or onything like that frae the kitchen, she puts yin o' the bools doon a pipe into the kitchen, and the stuff comes up wi' naething said."

'Whit dae ye ca' that game?' asks Duffy, lookin' at her pappin' doon the bools, 'it's no' moshy, onywye.'

'No, nor moshy,' I says to him. 'That's Art. Ye can hae yer pie frae the kitchen withoot them yellin' doon a pipe for't and lettin' a' the ither customers ken whit ye want.'

"When the pie cam' up, it was jist the shape o' an ordinary pie, wi' nae beads nor onything Art aboot it, and Duffy cheered up at that, and said he enjoyed his tea."

"I hope the refining and elevating influence of Miss Cranston's beautiful rooms will have a permanent effect on Duffy's taste," I said.

"Perhaps it will," said Erchie; "but we were nae sooner oot than he was wonderin' where the nearest place wad be for a gless o' beer."

XXIII

THE HIDDEN TREASURE

"I wish somebody would leave me some money," said Jinnet, "and the first thing I would dae wi't would be to buy ye a new topcoat. That yin's gettin' gey shabby, and that glazed, I can almaist see my face in the back o't."

"Then ye're weel aff," said Erchie, "for there's seldom ye'll see a bonnier yin in a better lookin'-gless."

"Oh, ye auld haver!" cried Jinnet, pushing him. "I wonder ye divna think shame to be talkin' like a laddie to his first lass, and me jist a done auld body! If I could jist get a shape I wad buy a remnant and mak' ye a topcoat mysel.' I could dae't quite easy."

"I ken that fine," said her husband, "but I'll bate ye would put the buttons on the wrang side, the wye ye did wi' yon waistcoat. It's a droll thing aboot weemen's claes that they aye hae their buttons on caurey-handed. It jist lets ye see their contrairiness."

"Oh! it's a peety ye mairried me," said Jinnet, "a contrairy wife must be an awfu' handfu'."

"Weel, so ye are contrairy," said Erchie firmly.

"It tak's twa to be contrairy, jist the same wye as it tak's twa to mak' a quarrel," said Jinnet, picking some fluff off his sleeve. "Whit wye am I contrairy I would like to ken?"

"If ye werena contrairy ye would be thinkin' o' buying' something for yersel' instead o' a topcoat for me, and ye're far mair needn't," said Erchie, and with that a knock came to the door.

"There's somebody," said Jinnet hastily; "put on the kettle."

★　　　★　　　★

"Come awa' in, Mr Duffy, and you, Mrs Duffy," said Jinnet, "we're rale gled to see ye, Erchie and me. I was jist puttin' on the kettle to mak' a drap tea."

Duffy and his wife came into the cosy light and warmth of the kitchen, and sat down. There was an elation in the coalman's eye that could not be concealed.

"My jove! I've news for ye the nicht," said he, taking out his pipe and lighting it.

"If it's that the bag o' coals is up anither bawbee," said Erchie, "there's nae hurry for't. It's no' awfu' new news that onywye."

"Ye needna be aye castin' up my tred to me," protested Duffy.

"Whaur would ye be wantin' coals?"

"Mr MacPherson's quite richt," said Mrs Duffy; "everybody kens it's no' an awfu' genteel thing sellin' coals, they're that—that black. I'm aye at him, Mrs MacPherson, to gie up the tred and the lorries and start a' eatin'-house. I could bake and cook for't fine. Noo that this money's comin' to us, we could dae't quite easy. Look at the profit aff mulk itsel'!"

"Dear me! hae ye come into a fortune?" cried Jinnet eagerly. "Isn't that droll? I was jist saying to Erchie that I wisht somebody would leave me something and I would buy him a new topcoat."

"That'll be a' richt," said Duffy. "If he'll gie him a haund wi' this thing I called aboot the nicht, I'll stand him the finest topcoat in Gleska, if it costs a pound."

"If it's ca'in on lawyers and the like o' that ye want me to dae," said Erchie, "I'm nae use to ye. I've a fine wye wi' me for ministers and the like o' that, that's no' aye wantin' to get the better o' ye, but lawyers is different. I yince went to a lawyer that was a member in oor kirk to ask him if he didna think it was time for him to pay his sate-rents. He said he would think it ower, and a week efter that he sent me an account for six-and-eightpence for consultation. But I'm prood to hear ye've come in for something, Duffy, whether I get a topcoat or no'. I never kent ye had ony rich freen's at a'. Faith, ye're well aff. Look at me, I havena a rich freen' in the warld except—except Jinnet."

"Oh, I never kent she was that weel aff," cried Mrs Duffy.

"Is it her!" said Erchie. "She has that much money in the bank that the bank clerks touch their hats to her in the street if she has on her Sunday claes. But that wasna whit I was thinkin' o'. There's ither kinds o' riches besides the sort they keep in banks."

"Never mind him, he's an auld fuiter," said Jinnet, spreading a tablecloth on the table and preparing for the tea. "I'm shair I'm gled to hear o' your good luck. It doesna dae to build oorsel's up on money, for money's no everything, as the pickpocket said when he took the watch as weel. But we're a' quite ready to thole't. Ye'll be plannin' whit ye'll dae wi't, Mrs Duffy?"

"First and foremost we're gaun to get rid o' the ree, at onyrate," said Mrs Duffy emphatically. "Then we're gaun to get a piano."

"Can ye play?" asked Erchie.

"No," admitted Mrs Duffy, "but there's nae need tae play sae lang's ye can get a vinolia to play for ye. I think we'll flit at the term to yin o' yon hooses roond the corner, wi' the tiled closes, and maybe keep a wee servant lassie. I'm that nervous at havin' to rise for the mulk in the mornin'. No' an awfu' big servant wi' keps and aiprons, ye understaund, but yin I could train into the thing. I'm no' for nane o' your late dinners. I jist like to tak' something in my hand for my supper."

"Och ay, ye'll can easy get a wee no' awfu' strong yin frae the country, chape," said Erchie. "Ye must tak' care o' yer ain health, Mrs Duffy, and if ye're nervous, risin' in the mornin' to tak' in the mulk's no' for ye. But my! ye'll no' be for speakin' to the like o' us when ye come into your fortune."

"It's no' exactly whit ye wad ca' a fortune," Duffy explained, as they drew in their chairs to the table. "But it's a heap o' money to get a' yince withoot daein' onything for't."

"Will ye hae to gang into mournin's for the body that left it?" Jinnet asked Mrs Duffy. "I ken a puir weedow wumman that would come to the hoose to sew for ye."

"Ye're aff it a'thegither," said Duffy. "It's naebody that left it to us—it's a medallion. Whit I wanted to ask ye, Erchie, is this—whit's a medallion?"

"Jist a kind o' a medal," said Erchie.

"My jove! said Duffy, "the wife was richt efter a'. I thocht it was something for playin' on, like a melodian. Weel, it doesna maitter, ye've heard o' the hidden treasure the newspapers is puttin' here and there round the country? I ken where yin o' them's hidden. At least I ken where there's a medallion."

"Oh, hoo nice!" said Jinnet. "It's awfu' smert o' ye, Mr Duffy. I was jist readin' aboot them, and was jist hopin' some puir body wad get them."

"No' that poor naither!" said Mrs Duffy, with a little warmth.

"Na, na, I wasna sayin'——I didna mean ony hairm," said poor Jinnet. "Streetch yer hand, and tak' a bit cake. That's a rale nice brooch ye hae gotten."

Erchie looked at Duffy dubiously. For a moment he feared the coalman might be trying on some elaborate new kind of joke, but the complacency of his face put it out of the question.

"Then my advice to you, Duffy, if ye ken where the medallion is," said Erchie, "is to gang and howk it up at yince, or somebody 'll be there afore ye. I warrant it'll no' get time to tak' root if it's within a penny ride on the Gleska skoosh cars. There's thoosands o' people oot wi' lanterns at this very meenute scrapin' dirt in the hunt for that medallion. Hoo do ye ken whaur it is if ye havena seen it?"

"It's there richt enough," said Mrs Duffy, "it's in the paper, and we're gaun to gie up the ree. My mind's made up on that. I hope ye'll come and see us sometime in our new hoose—house."

"It says in the paper," said Duffy, "that the medallion's up a street that has a public-hoose at each end o't, and a wee pawn in the middle, roond the corner o' anither street, where ye can see twa laundries at yince, and a sign ower yin o' them that puts ye in mind o' the battle o' Waterloo. Then, in a parteecular place, twenty yairds to the richt o' a pend-close wi' a barrow in't."

Erchie laughed. "Wi' a barrow in't?" said he. "They micht as weel hae said wi' a polisman in't. Barrows is like bobbies—if ye think ye'll get them where ye want them, ye're up a close yersel'. And whit's the parteecular place, Duffy?"

Duffy leaned forward and whispered mysteriously, "MY COAL-REE."

"But we're gaun to gie't up," explained his wife. "Oh, ay, we're gaun to give the ree up. Ye hae no idea whaur—where—I could get a smert wee lassie that would not eat awfu' much, Mrs MacPherson?"

"I measured it a' aff," Duffy went on. "It's oor street richt enough. The pubs is there——"

"——I could bate ye they are," said Erchie. "If they werena there it wad be a miracle."

"——and the laundries is there. 'Colin Campbell' ower yin o' them, him that bate Bonypart, ye ken, and twenty yairds frae the pend-close is richt under twenty ton o' coal I put in last week. It's no McCallum's wid-yaird, it's my ree."

"My papa was the sole proprietor of a large wid-yaird," irrelevantly remarked Mrs Duffy, who was getting more and more Englified as the details of the prospective fortune came out.

"Was he, indeed," said Jinnet. "That was nice!"

"Noo, whit I wanted you to dae for me," Duffy went on, "was to come awa' doon wi' me the nicht and gie's a hand to shift thae coals. I daurna ask ony o' my men to come, for they wad claim halfers."

Erchie toyed with a teaspoon and looked at the coalman, half in pity, half with amusement. "Man, ye're a rale divert," said he at last. "Do ye think the newspapers would be at the bother o' puttin' their medallion under twenty ton o' coal in your coal-ree, or onybody else's? Na, na, they can mak' their money easier than that. If ye tak' my advice, ye'll put a penny on the bag o' coal and gie short wecht, and ye'll mak' your fortune far shairer than lookin' under't for medallions."

"Then ye're no' game to gie's a hand?" said Duffy, starting another cookie. "See's the sugar."

"Not me!" said Erchie promptly. "I've a flet fit and a warm hert, but I'm no' a'thegither a born idiot to howk coal for medallions that's no' there."

★　　　★　　　★

Next day Duffy came up with two bags of coals which Jinnet had ordered.

"Did ye find the medallion? she asked him.

"I didna need to look for't," he replied. "I heard efter I left here last nicht that a man found it in a back-coort in the Garscube Road. Them sort of dydoes should be put doon by the polis."

"Oh, whit a peety!" said Jinnet. "And hoo's the mistress the day?"

"She's fine," said Duffy. "She's ca'in' me Jimmy again; it was naething but Mr Duffy wi' her as lang's she thocht we were to get rid o' the ree."

XXIV

THE VALENTEEN

On the night of the last Trades House dinner I walked home with Erchie when his work was done. It was the 13th of February. There are little oil-and-colour shops in New City Road, where at that season the windows became literary and artistic, and display mock valentines. One of these windows caught my old friend's eye, and he stopped to look in.

"My!" he said, "time flies! It was only yesterday we had the last o' oor Ne'erday currant-bun, and here's the valenteens! That minds me I maun buy——" He stopped and looked at me, a little embarrassed.

I could only look inquiry back at him.

"Ye'll think I'm droll," said he, "but it just cam' in my heid to buy a valenteen. To-morrow's Jinnet's birthday, and it would be a rale divert to send her ladyship yin and tak' a kind o' rise oot o' her. Come and gie's a hand to pick a nice yin."

I went into the oil-and-colour shop, but, alas! for the ancient lover, he found there that the day of sentiment was done so far as the 14th of February was concerned.

Hae ye ony nice valenteens?" he asked a boy behind the counter.

"Is't a comic ye mean?" asked the boy, apparently not much amazed at so strange an application from an elderly gentleman.

"A comic!" said my friend in disdain. "Dae I look like the kind o' chap that sends mock valenteens? If ye gie me ony o' your chat I'll tell yer mither, ye wee—ye wee rascal! Ye'll be asking me next if I want a mooth harmonium. Dae ye think I'm angry wi' the cook in some hoose roond in the terraces because she's chief wi' the letter-carrier? I'll comic ye!"

"Weel, it's only comics we hae," said the youthful shopkeeper, "the only ither kind we hae 's Christmas cairds, and I think we're oot o' them."

He was a business-like boy—he flung a pile of the mock valentines on the counter before us.

Erchie turned them over with contemptuous fingers. "It's a gey droll age we live in," said he to me. "We're far ower funny, though ye wadna think it to see us. I have a great respect for valenteens, for if it wasna for a valenteen there maybe wadna hae been ony Jinnet—at least in my hoose, I wad gie a shillin' for a rale auld-

102

fashioned valenteen that gaed oot and in like a concertina, wi' lace roond aboot it, and smell o' scent aff it, and twa silver herts on't skewered through the middle the same as it was for brandering. Ye havena seen mony o' that kind, laddie? Na, I daursay no'. There were oot afore your time, though I thocht ye micht hae some in the back-shop. They were the go when we werena nearly sae smert as we are nooadays. I'm gled I havena to start the coortin' again."

He came on one of the garish sheets that was less vulgar than the others, with the picture of a young lady under an umbrella, and a verse of not unkindly doggerel.

"That'll hae to dae," said he, "although it's onything but fancy."

"I hope," said I dubiously, "that Mrs MacPherson will appreciate it."

"She's the very yin that will," he assured me, as he put it in his pocket. "She's like mysel', she canna play the piano, but she has better gifts—she has the fear o' God and a sense o' humour. You come up the morn's nicht at eight, afore the post comes, and ye'll see the ploy when she gets her valenteen. I'll be slippin' oot and postin't in the forenoon. Though a young lassie canna get her valenteens ower early in the mornin', a mairried wife's 'll dae very weel efter her wark's done for the day."

"It's yersel'?" said Mrs MacPherson when I went to her door. "Come awa' in. I kent there was a stranger comin'—though indeed I wadna be ca'in' you a stranger—for there was a stranger on the ribs o' the grate this mornin', and a knife fell aff the table when we were at oor tea."

"Ay, and who knocked it aff deeliberate?" interposed her husband, rising to welcome me. "Oh, she's the sly yin. She's that fond to see folk come aboot the hoose she whiles knocks a knife aff the table to see if it'll bring them."

"Oh, Erchie MacPherson!" cried his wife.

"I'm no' blamin' ye," he went on, "I ken I'm gey dreich company for onybody. I havena a heid for mindin' ony scandal aboot the folk we ken, and I canna understaund politics noo that Gledstone's no' to the fore, and I canna sing, or play a tune on onything."

"Listen to him!" cried Jinnet. "Isn't he the awfu' man? Did ye ever hear the like o' him for nonsense?"

The kettle was on the fire. I knew from experience that it had been put there when my knock came to the door, for so the good lady's hospitality always manifested itself, so that her kettle was off and on the fire a score of times a-day, ready to be brought to the boil if it was a visitor who knocked, and not a beggar or a pedlar of pipeclay.

"Tak' a watter biscuit," Jinnet pressed me as we sat at the table, "they're awfu' nice wi' saut butter."

"Hae ye nae syrup to put on them?" asked her husband with a sly glance.

"Nane o' yer nonsense," she exclaimed, and attempted a diversion in the conversation, but Erchie plainly had a joke to retail.

"I'll tell ye a baur aboot watter biscuits and syrup," said he. "When I was coortin' my first lass I wasna mair than nineteen years o' age, and jist a thin peely-wally callent, mair like playin' moshy at the bools than rinnin' efter lassies. The lassie's faither and mither jist made fun o' us, and when I wad be gaun up to her hoose, lettin' on it was her brither I wanted to see, they used to affront me afore their dochter wi' speakin' aboot the Sunday School and the Band o' Hope I belanged to (because the lassie belanged to them tae), and askin' me if I was fond o' sugar to my parridge, and when I was thinkin' o' startin' the shavin'. I didna like it, but I jist had to put up wi't. But the worst blow ever I got frae them was yince when I gaed up wi' a new pair o' lavender breeks, and the lassie's mither, for the fun o' the thing, asked me if I wad hae a piece and jeely. I tellt her I wasna needin', that I was jist efter haein' my tea, but she went and spread syrup on a watter biscuit and handed it to me the same as if I was a wee lauddie wi' a grauvit on."

Jinnet laughed softly at the picture.

"Oh, ye may laugh," said her husband. "There was nae laughin' in my heid, I'm tellin' ye. For there was the syrup comin' dreepin' through the holes in the watter biscuit, so that I had to haud the biscuit up every noo and then and lick it below't so as to keep the syrup frae gaun on my braw lavender breeks. A bonny object for a lass to look at, and it was jist to mak' me look reediculous her mither did it. She thocht I was faur ower young to be comin' efter her dochter."

"So ye were," said Jinnet. "I'm shair ye hadna muckle sense at the time, or it wadna be yon yin ye went coortin'."

"Maybe no'; but I never rued it," said Erchie.

"She was as glaikit as yersel'," said Jinnet.

"She was the cleverest lass in the place," protested Erchie. "My!

the things she could sew, and crochet, and mak' doon, and bake!"

"Her sister Phemie was faur cleverer than she was," said Jinnet. "She couldna haud a candle to her sister Phemie in tambourin' or in gingerbreid."

"And dancin'! She could dance on a cobweb and no' put a toe through't."

"Ye'll need a line wi' that yin, Erchie," said his wife, who did not seem remarkably jealous of this first love.

"Ye should hear her singin'——"

"She wad hae been far better mendin' her wee brither's stockin's, and no' leavin' her mither to dae't," said Jinnet. "She was gey licht-heided yin."

Erchie seemed merciless in his reminiscence,—I really felt sorry for his wife.

"Ye may say whit ye like to run her doon, but ye canna deny her looks."

"Her looks dinna concern me." said Jinnet abruptly. "Ye're jist an auld haver. Think shame o' yersel'!"

"Ye ken ye canna deny't," he went on. "It was alooed all over the place she was the belle. I wasna the only yin that was efter her wi' my lavender breeks. She kept the Band o' Hope for nearly twa years frae burstin' up."

"I'll no' listen to anither word," protested Jinnet, now in obvious vexation and, mercifully, there came a rapping at the door.

She returned to the kitchen with an envelope and a little parcel. Erchie winked at me, hugging to himself a great delight.

"I wonder wha in the world can be writin' to me," said she, looking at the addresses.

"It'll likely be an accoont for di'mond tararas or dressmaking," said Erchie. "Oh you weemen! Ye're a perfect ruination. But if I was you I wad open them and see."

She opened the envelope first. It was Erchie's valentine, and she knew it, for when she read the verse she shook her head at him laughingly, and a little ashamed. "When will ye be wise?" she said.

Then she opened the little parcel. It contained a trivial birthday gift from an anonymous friend in whose confidence only I, of all the three in the room, happened to be. Vainly they speculated about his identity without suspecting me, but I noticed that it was on her valentine Jinnet set most value. She held it long in her hand, thinking, and was about to put it into a chest of drawers without letting me see it.

"Ye needna be hidin' it," said her husband then. "He saw it already. Faith! he helped me to pick it."

"I'm fair affronted," she exclaimed, reddening at this exposure. "You and your valenteens!"

"There's naething wrang wi' valenteens," said her husband. "If it wasna for a valenteen I wad never hae got ye. I could never say to your face but that I liked ye, but the valenteen had a word that's far mair brazen than 'like,' ye mind."

"Oh, Erchie!" I cried, "you must have been blate in these days. The word was——"

He put up his hand in alarm and stopped me. "Wheesht! said he. "It's a word that need never be mentioned here where we're a' three Scotch!"

"But what came over the first lass, Erchie?" I asked determined to have the end of that romance.

He looked across at his wife and smiled. "She's there hersel'," said he, "and ye better ask her."

"What! Jinnet?" I cried, amazed at my own obtuseness.

"Jinnet of course," said he. "Wha else wad it be if it wasna Jinnet? She's the Rale Oreeginal."

XXV
AMONG THE PICTURES

"Whaur are ye gaun the day?" said Erchie to Duffy on Saturday afternoon when he came on the worthy coalman standing at his own close-mouth, looking up and down the street with the hesitation of a man who deliberates how he is to make the most of his Saturday half-holiday.

"I was just switherin'," said Duffy. "Since I got mairried and stopped gaun to the Mull o' Kintyre Vaults, there's no' much choice for a chap. I micht as weel be leevin' in the country for a' the life I see."

"Man, aye!" said Erchie," that's the warst o' Gleska, there's nae life in't—naethin' daein'. Ye should try yer hand at takin' oot the wife for a walk, jist for the novelty o' the thing."

"Catch me!" said Duffy. "She wad see ower mony things in the shop windows she was needin'. I was jist wonderin' whether I wad buy a 'Weekly Mail' or gang to the fitba' match at Parkheid."

Erchie looked pityingly at him. "A fitba' match!" said he. "Whit's the use o' gaun to a fitba' match when ye can see a' aboot it in the late edeetion? Forbye, a fitba' match doesna improve the mind. It's only sport. I'll tell ye whit I'll dae wi' ye if ye're game. I'll tak' ye to the Art Institute. The minister gied me twa tickets. Awa' and put on your collar and I'll wait here on ye."

"Do ye need a collar for the gallery?" asked Duffy who thought the Art Institute was a music-hall. On this point Erchie set him right, and, ten minutes later, with a collar whose rough edges rasped his neck and made him unhappy, he was on his way to Sauchiehall Street.

The band was playing a waltz tune as they entered the Institute. "Mind, I'm no' on for ony dancin'," Duffy explained. "I canna be bothered dancin'."

"There's naebody gaun to ask ye to dance," said Erchie, "Do you think there couldna be a baun' playin' withoot dancin'? It's jist here to cod a lot o' folk into the notion that they can be cheery enough in a place o' this kind, in spite o' the pictures. And ye can get aifternoon tea here, too."

"I could be daein' wi' a gless o' beer," said Duffy.

"No. They're no' that length yet." Erchie explained. "There's only the tea. The mair determined lovers o' the Fine Arts can dae the hale

107

show in an aifternoon noo wi' the help o' a cup o' tea, so that they needna come back again. It's a great savin'. They used to hae to gang hame for their tea afore, and whiles they never got back. The Institute wasna popular in thae days. It was that quate and secluded that if a chap had done onything wrang and the detectives were efter him he took a season ticket, and spent a' his days here. Noo, ye can see for yersel' the place is gaun like an inn. That's the effect o' the baun' and the aifternoon tea. If they added a baby incubator to the attractions the same's they hae in the East-End Exhibeetion, they would need the Fire Brigade wi' a hose to keep the croods oot. Ye hae nae idea o' the fascination Art has for the people o' Gleska if they're no' driven to't."

"My jove!" exclaimed Duffy, at the sight of the first gallery. "Whit a lot o' pictures! There'll be a pile o' money in a place o' this kind. Hiv they no water-shoot, or a shootin' jungle, or onything lively like that?"

"Man, ye're awfu' common, whiles, Duffy," said Erchie. "I'm fear't I wasted my ticket on ye. This is no' an ordinary show for haein' fun at. It's for enlargin' the mind, opening' the e'en to the beauties o' nature, and sellin' pictures."

"Are they a' for sale?" asked Duffy, looking with great intentness at a foggy impression by Sidaner, the French artist.

"No' the hale o' them, there's some on lend."

"I could hae lent them a topper," said Duffy,—"faur aheid o' onything here. It's a drawin' o' a horse I yince had in my first lorry. It was pented for me by a penter that lodged above us, and had a great name for sign-boards. it cost me nearly a pound wan wye or anither, though I provided the pent mysel'."

"Ay, Art's a costly thing," said Erchie. "Ye'll seldom get a good picture under a pound. It's no' a'thegither the pent, it's the layin' o't on by hand."

"This yin's done by hand onywye," said Duffy, pointing to the foggy impression by Sidaner. "It's awfu' like as if somebody had done it themsel's in their spare time."

"You and me's no' judges o' that sort o' thing," said Erchie. "Maybe it's no' near so bad as it looks."

"Ye see," Erchie went on, "Art pentin's a tred by itsel'. There used to be hardly ony picture-penters in Gleska. It was a' shipbuildin' and calanderin', whatever that is, and chemical works that needed big lums. When a Gleska man did a guid stroke o' business on the Stock

108

Exchange, or had money left him in thae days, and his wife wanted a present, he had his photygraph ta'en big size, ile-coloured by hand. It was gey like him, the photygraph, and so everybody kent it wasna the rale Art. Folk got rich that quick in Gleska, and had sae much money to spend, that the photygraphers couldna keep up wi' the demand, and then the hand-pentin' chaps began to open works in different pairts o' the city. Ye'll hardly gang into a hoose noo whaur ye'll no' see the guidman's picture in ile, and it micht be bilin' ile sometimes, judgin' from the agony on his face."

"My jove!" said Duffy, "is it sore to get done that wye?"

"Sore!" replied Erchie; "no, nor sore. At least, no' that awfu' sore. They wadna need to dae't unless they liked. When maistly a' the weel-aff Gleska folk had got their photygraphs done and then de'ed, the penters had to start the landscape brench o' the business. Them's landscapes a' roon' aboot"—and Erchie gave his arm a comprehensive sweep to suggest all the walls.

"They must be pretty smert chaps that does them," said Duffy. "I wish I had gone in for the pentin' mysel'. It's cleaner than the coals. Dae ye hae to serve your time?"

"No, nor time; ye can see for yersel' that it's jist a kind o' knack like poetry—or waitin'. And the plant doesna cost much. A' ye need to start wi' is paper, brushes, pent, and a saft hat."

"A saft hat!"

"Aye, a saft hat's the sure sign o' an artist. I ken hunners o' them. Gleska's fair hotchin' wi' artists. If the Cairters' Trip wasna abolished, ye wad see the artists' tred union walkin' oot wi' the rest o' them."

The two friends went conscientiously round the rooms, Erchie expounding on the dimensions, frames, and literary merits of the pictures, Duffy a patient, humble student, sometimes bewildered at the less obvious transcripts of nature and life pointed out to him.

"Is there much mair o' this to see?" he asked at last, after having gone through the fourth gallery. "I'm gettin' dizzy. Could we no' hae something at the tea bar if we gied them a tip? They micht send oot for't. Or we micht get a pass-oot check."

"Mair to see!" exclaimed Erchie. "Ye're awfu' easy made dizzy! The like o' you wad faur raither be oot skreichin' yer heid aff at the fitba' match at Parkheid, instead o' improvin' the mind here. Ye canna get onything at the tea place but jist tea, I'm tellin' ye, and there's nae pass-oot checks. They ken better than to gie ye pass-oot checks. Haulf o' your kind wad never come back again if yince ye escaped."

"My jove!" said Duffy, suddenly, "here's a corker!" and he indicated a rather peculiar drawing with a lady artist's name attached to it.

Erchie himself was staggered. "It's ca'd 'The Sleeper' in the catalogue," said he. "It's a wumman, and she's dozin'. The leddy that pented it wasna ower lavish wi' her pent. That's whit they ca' New Art, Duffy. It jist shows ye whit weemen can dae if ye let them."

"And dae ye tell me there's weemen penters?" asked Duffy in astonishment.

"Of course there's weemen penters."

"And hoo dae they get up and doon ladders?" asked Duffy.

"I'm tellin' ye, Art pentin's a branch by itsel'," said Erchie. "The Lady Art penters divna pent windows, and rhones and hooses. They bash brass, and hack wud, and draw pictures."

"And can they mak' a living at that?"

"Whiles. And whiles their paw helps."

"My jove!" said Duffy, bewildered.

"We'll gang on to the next room noo," said Erchie.

"I wad raither come back some ither day," said Duffy. "I'm enjoyin' this fine, but I promised the wife I wad be hame early for my tea." And together they hastily made an exit into Sauchiehall Street.

"I wonder wha won the semi-final at Parkheid," said Duffy. "We'll awa' doon the toon and see. Whit's the use o' hurryin' hame?"

110

XXVI

THE PROBATIONARY GHOST

One day I observed Erchie going off the pavement rather than walk under a ladder.

"And are you superstitious too?" I asked him, surprised at this unsuspected trait in a character so generally sensible.

"I don't care whither ye ca't supersteetion or no'," he replied, "but walkin' under ladders is a gey chancy thing, and there's mony a chancy thing, I'm neither that young nor that weel aff that I can afford to be takin' ony risks."

"Dear me!" I said; "I wouldn't be surprised to learn that you believed in ghosts."

"Do I no'?" he answered. "And guid reason for't! Did I no' yince see yin? It was the time I had the rheumatic fever, when we were stayin' in Garnethill. I was jist gettin' better, and sittin' up a wee while in the evenin' to air the bed, and Jinnet was oot for a message. The nicht was wild and wet, and the win' was daudin' awa' at the window like onything, and I was feelin' gey eerie, and wearyin' for the wife to come back. I was listenin' for her fit on the stair, when the ootside door opens, and in a second there was a chap at the kitchen door.

"Come in if your feet's clean,' says I, pretty snappy. 'Seein' ye've made sae free wi' the ae door ye needna mak' ony ceremony wi' this ane.' I heard the hinges screechin.' but naebody cam' in, and I looks roon' frae where I was sittin' wi' a blanket roond me at the fire, and there was the ghost keekin' in' He was a wee nyaf o' a thing, wi' a Paisley whisker, a face no bigger than a Geneva watch, a nickerbocker suit on, Rab Roy tartan tops to his gowfin' stockings, and pot-bellied to the bargain. I kent fine he was a ghost at the first gae-aff."

'It's you,' says I. 'Come in and gies yer crack till Jinnet comes. Losh, it's no' a nicht for stravaigin'.'

"He cam' glidin' in withoot makin' ony soond at a', and sat doon on a chair."

'Ye're no' feared,' says he, trying to gnash his teeth, and makin' a puir job o't, for they were maistly arteeficial.

'Feared?' says I. 'No me! I never did onybody ony hairm that wad mak' it worth ony ghost's while to meddle wi' me. A flet fit but a warm hert.'

'We'll see aboot that,' says he, as cocky as onything. 'I had a fine job findin' oot whaur ye were. Fancy me gaun awa' doon to Millport on a nicht like this to haunt ye, and findin' that ye had flitted up here last term.' And he begood to gnash his teeth again.

'Millport!' says I. 'Man! I was never near the place, and I've lived in this hoose for seventeen year, and brocht up a faimily in't.'

"I never seen a ghost mair vexed than he was when I tell't him that. His jaw fell. He was nearly greetin'.

'Whit's yer name?' he asked.

'Erchie MacPherson, and I'm no' ashamed o't. It's no' in ony grocers' nor tylers' books that I ken o', and if I ever murdered ony weans or onything o' that sort, it must hae been when I was sleepin'. I doot, my man, ye're up the wrang close.'

"The ghost begood to swear. Oh my! such swearin'. I never listened to the bate o't. There was fancy words in't I never heard in a' my life, and I've kent a wheen o' cairters."

'That's jist like them,' says he. 'They tellt me Millport, and efter I couldna find the man I was wantin' at Millport, I was tellt it was here, No. 16 Buccleuch Street. Fancy me bungin' awa' through the air on a nicht like this! My nicker-bockers is fair stickin' to my knees wi' wet.'

'Peter,' says I (of course I didna ken his richt name, but I thocht I wad be nice wi' the chap seein' he had made such a mistake), 'Peter,' said I, 'ye're needin' yer specs on. This is no' No. 16, it's No. 18, and I think the man ye maun be lookin' for is Jeckson, that canvasses for the sewin-machines. He came here last term frae aboot Millport. If he's done ony hairm to onybody in his past life— murdered a wife, and buried her under the hearth-stane, or ony daft-like thing o' that sort—I'm no' wantin' to hear onything aboot it, for he's a guid enough neebour, has twa bonny wee weans, comes hame regular to his tea, and gangs to the kirk wi' his wife. He's been teetotal ever since he came here. Gie the chap a chance!'

'Jeckson!' said the ghost, and whips oot a wee book.

That's the very man!' said he. 'Man! is't no' aggravatin? Here's me skooshin' up and doon the coast wi' my thin flannels on lookin' for him, and him toastin' his taes at a fire in Buccleuch Street! Jist you wait. It shows ye the wye the books in oor place is kept. If the office was richt up-to-date, Jeckson wadna be flitted ten meenutes when his new address wad be marked doon. No wonder the Americans is batin' us! Weel, it's no' my faut if I'm up the wrang close, and i'm no' gaun to start the job the nicht. I'm far ower cauld.'

"There was an empty gless and a teaspoon on the dresser, for Jinnet had been giein' me a drap toddy afore she gaed oot. The ghost sat doon on a chair and looked at the gless."

'Could ye save a life?' said he.

'Whit wad be the use o' giein' it to you, Peter?' I asked him, 'ye havena ony inside, seein' ye're a ghost.'

'Have I no'?' says he. 'Jist try me.' So I pointed to the press, and he took oot the decanter as smert's ye like and helped himsel'.

"He turned oot a rale nice chap in spite o' his tred, and he gave me a' the oot and ins o't. 'I've nae luck,' he said. 'It's my first job at the hauntin', and I've made a kind o' botch o't, though it's no my faut. I'm a probationer, jist on my trial, like yin o' thae U.F. ministers. Maybe ye think it's easy gettin' a haunter's job, but I'm tellin' ye it's no' that easy. And when ye get it, it's wark that tak's it oot o' ye. There's mair gangs in for the job there than for the Ceevil Service here, and the jobs go to compeetition. Ye hae to pass an examination, and ye hae nae chance o' gettin' yin if ye divna mak' mair than ninety per cent. o' points. Mind ye, there's mair than jist plain ghost-wark. It used to be, in the auld days, that a haunter wad be sent to dae onything—to rattle chains, or gie ye the clammy hand, or be a blood-curdler. Nooadays there's half a dizzen different kinds o' haunters. I'm a blood-curdler mysel',' and he gied a skreich that nearly broke a' the delf on the dresser.

'Nane o' that!' says I, no' very well pleased. 'Ye'll hae the neebours doon on us. Forbye, there's naething patent aboot that sort o' skreich. Duffy the coalman could dae better himsel'. That's no' the wye a decent ghost should cairry on in ony hoose whaur he's gettin' a dram'.

'Excuse me,' he says; 'it's the dram that's ta'en my heid. Ye see, I'm no' used to't. It's mony a day since I had yin.'

'Are they that strict yonder?' I asked.

'Strict's no' the word for't! If a blood-curdler on probation was kent to gang to his work wi' the smell o' drink aff him, he wad lose his job', and he helped himsel' to anither dram.

'Weel, ye're no' blate onywye,' says I.

'Blate! Catch me,' says he. 'I wadna need to be blate at this tred, I'm tellin' ye. Jist you think o' the kind o' customers we hae to dale wi'! They wad sooner see a tax-collector comin' into their hooses than yin o' us chaps. There's some hooses ye hae to gang to work in where it's easy. I ken a ghost that's been fifteen years on the same job, and gettin' fat on't. He has the name o' bein' the best white-sheet ghost in the Depairtmen', and he's stationed in an auld castle up aboot the Hielan's, a job he got because he had the Gaelic. He made it sae hot for the folk, walkin' aboot their bedrooms at a' 'oors o' the nicht, that naebody 'll stay in the place but himsel' and an auld deaf and dumb housekeeper. There's naething for him to dae, so he can lie in his bed a' nicht and no' bother himsel' aboot onything. It's a very different thing wi' anither chap I ken—a chain-clanker in England. He has to drag ten yairds o' heavy chain up and doon stairs every nicht, and it's no easy job, I'm tellin' ye, wi' the folk the hoose belang to pappin' things and shootin' at whaur they think the soond comes frae. Oh ay! there's a great run on the best jobs. My ain embeetion is to be in the clammy-hand brench o' the business in some quate wee place at the coast. I hae my e'e on likely thing at Rothesay. Of course the clammy hand's no' a very nice occupation for the winter, but this is a hoose that's shut up in the winter, and I wad only hae to work it in the fine summer nichts."

'Hoo dae ye dae the clammy hand, Peter?' I asked him, and he just winked.

'If I was tellin' ye that,' says he, 'ye wad be as wise as mysel'. Never you mind, MacPherson. Ask me nae questions and I'll tell ye nae lees. Weel, as I was sayin', I aye had a notion o' a quate job at the coast. I couldna stand Gleska. There's such a rush aboot it, and sae mony stairs to sclim, and pianos aye playin' next door. And the accent's awfu'! Gie me a nice wee country hoose whaur somebody hanged himsel', wi' roses on the wa', and dandelions in the front plot. But there's plenty o' us lookin' efter jobs o' that sort—far ower mony. And it's generally them wi' influence that gets them at the hinner-end.'

'That's whit everybody says aboot the situations here, Peter,' says I. 'If they're nae use at their tred they talk a lot aboot influence. I'm thinkin' ye wad soon get a job at the coast if ye were fit for't.'

"He was the shortest-tempered ghost ever I seen. I had nae sooner said that than he gied anither skreich, and disappeared in a blue lowe wi' an awfu' smell o' brimstone."

'Come oot o' that!' I says to him, 'I can see the taps o' yer gowfin' stockings', and at that he gied a kind o' shamed laugh and was sittin' in the chair again, helpin' himsel' to anither dram.

'I'll tell ye whit I'll dae wi' ye,' said he. 'I'll no' mind aboot Jeckson at a', but I'll hing aboot your hoose for a week or a fortnight, and they'll never ken at the office. I canna think to gang into Jackson's hoose if he's a teetotaler. Tee-totalers is aye that—that—that teetotal. I wad never get sittin' doon in Jeckson's to a jovial gless like this.'

'Ye're far ower jovial for me,' says I. 'See's that decanter,' and I took it frae him. 'I'm awfu' prood to see ye, but ye better be slidin' afore her ladyship, the wife, comes in, or she'll put the hems on ye. She canna stand ghosts.'

'Mighty!' said he, 'have ye a wife?'

'The nicest wee wife in Gleska,' said I. 'And I wish to goodness she was hame, for I'm awfu' tired.'

'Then I'm no' playin',' said the ghost. 'I'll awa' roon' and gie Jeckson a cry afore he gangs to his bed.'

"He grabbed the decanter and emptied it into the tumbler, gied ae gulp, and anither gnash to his teeth, and went awa' withoot sae much as 'thenk ye.'

"Jinnet's step was on the stair. Fine I kent it! Man, that's the smertest wee wumman!"

'There's nae livin' in this hoose wi' ghosts,' says I to her when she cam' in, and she had some grapes for me.

'Is there no', Erchie?' she said, lookin' at me, 'my ain puir auld man!'

'Look at that decanter,' says I, 'the rascal emptied it.'

"'Hoots! the decanter's a' richt,' says she, takin't frae the press, and as shair's onything, there wasna a drap oot o't!

"And she put me to my bed there and then."

XXVII

JINNET's CHRISTMAS SHOPPING

Jinnet had money in the Savings Bank. Erchie used to chuckle when some neighbour had gone out to whom she had casually mentioned the fact and say, "That's it, Jinnet, you be bragging o' your deposits like that, and they'll be thinking I mairried ye for your fortune." But the truth was that when their savings at first were lodged in Erchie's name, they had an unfortunate way of disappearing without Jinnet's knowledge, and it was to protect himself from himself that the husband finally opened the account in the name of his wife.

The first day she went to the bank with money it was with no little trepidation. "Maybe they'll no' tak' sae much as twenty-wan pounds," she suggested; "it's a guid pickle money to hae the responsibility o'."

"Ay, and gled to get it!" he replied. "That's whit they're there for. If it was twice twenty-wan they wad mak' room for't even if they had to shift forrit the coonter. Ye hae nae idea o' the decency o' thae banks!"

"But whit if the bank was to burst?" said Jinnet. "Lots o' folk losses their money wi' banks burstin', and hae to go on the Board a' the rest o' their days."

"Burst!" laughed Erchie. "Man!" ye wad think it was a kitchen biler ye were talkin' aboot. It'll no' burst wi' a' we'll put into it. I'll warrant ye."

"Will ye hae to pay them much for takin' care o't?" she asked, still dubious of these immense financial operations.

Erchie laughed till the tears ran into his tea.

"Oh, my!" said he, "but ye're the caution! It's them that pays you. If ye leave the twenty-wan pound in for a twelvemonth, they'll gie ye something like twenty-wan pound ten shillin's when ye gang to lift it."

This troubled Jinnet worse than ever. "It's rale nice o' them," said she, "but I'm no' needin' their ten shillin's. We're no' that faur doon in the warld, and it's like enough they wad jist be takin' it aff some ither puir cratur."

But eventually the money was lodged in Jinnet's name. She used to take out her bank-book and examine it once a week, to make sure, as she said, 'the money was still there,' a proceeding at which Erchie would wink to himself, and with difficulty restrain his laughter.

On Saturday Jinnet expressed a wish that she had some of her money to make some purchases for Christmas and the New Year.

"Weel," said her husband, "whit's to hinder ye gaun to the bank and liftin' a pound or twa?"

Her face turned white at the very thought. "Me!" she cried. "I wadna ask for money at that bank if I was stervin'."

"But, bless my sowl! it's yer ain money. They canna keep ye frae gettin' it if ye want it," said her husband.

"I'm no carin'," Jinnet protested. "I divna like to ask for't, and them maybe busy. Perhaps the puir craturs havena got it to spare the noo."

"Weel, they can jist send oot for a wee lend o't frae somebody they ken," said Erchie. "It's your money, and if ye want ony o't oot they must gie ye't. That's whit banks is for."

"Will you no' gang for the twa pound ten for me, and I'll mak' something nice and tasty for your tea the nicht?" said Jinnet coaxingly. But Erchie had his own way of teaching Jinnet self-confidence, and refused. "They wadna gie't to me withoot a lot o' palaver," he explained; "ye'll just hae to gang yersel'. Speak nice to them, and they'll no' touch ye. There hasna been a customer murdered in a Gleska bank for years and years." He explained the process she was to follow, and she set out with great misgivings.

"Weel, hoo did ye get on?" Erchie asked her when she returned. "Ye got the money onywye—I can see by the wye yer nief's shut."

"Oh, Erchie!" she cried hysterically, and dropped into a chair. "I wad never mak' a man o' business. My hert's in a palpitation—jist fair stottin'. I peety them that has the bother o' muckle money."

"My jove!" said Erchie in alarm, "were they no' nice to ye? If they werena nice and ceevil, I'll—I'll tak' oot every penny, and then they'll see whaur they are."

"Oh, they were as nice as they could be," Jinnet hurried to explain. "And I got the money a' richt. But oh! I was that put-aboot. Thon slippy floor aye frichtens me, and the gentlemen inside the coonter in their wee cages like Duffy's goldy——"

"Goldies—ay, that's jist whit they are," said Erchie. "It's a fine bird a goldie if ye get a guid yin. It can whustle better than a canary."

"——like Duffy's goldie, and that rale well put-on. Each o' them had as muckle gold and silver aboot him as wad fill a bakie. I nearly fented when yin o' them spoke to me awfu' Englified, and askit whit he could dae for me the day. 'Oh,' says I, 'I see ye're throng. I'll can come back anither time,' and I was makin' for the door when he cried me back, and said he wasna that throng but that he wad be gled to dae onything he could for me. I thocht he wad gie me the money wi' a grudge when he found I wanted twa pound ten in silver, but he coonted it oot like lichtnin', and bangs if fornent me. A rale obleegin' lad he was, but no' lookin' awfu' strong. I think I'll knit him a pair o' warm socks or a muffler for his New Year."

"Ye're a rale divert, Jinnet!" said Erchie.

"I jist picked up the money withoot coontin' it and turned to gang awa'. Hold on, Mistress MacPherson,' he cries; 'ye'll be as weel to coont yer siller afore ye leave the bank in case I'm cheatin' ye,' and my face got as red's the fire. 'I wadna hae the cheek to doot ye efter seein' ye coontin't yersel',' I tellt him, and cam' awa'. But I went up a close further along the street and coonted it."

"I could bate a pound ye did," said Erchie.

And now, having got out her money, Jinnet had to go shopping. Ordinary shopping had no terrors for her. She loved to drop into Lindsay, the grocer's and discourse upon the prices of simple things to eat, and feel important when he offered to send his boy with the goods. She was quite at home in the little side-street shops where they sell trimming, and bolts of tape, and remnants of print, or the oil-and-colour shops where she was known and could spend a pleasant ten minutes' gossip over the purchase of a gallon of paraffin. But Christmas shopping was no ordinary shopping, and was entered on with almost as much apprehension as her expedition to the bank. It had to be done in big warehouses, where the attendants were utter strangers to her, and had ways frigid and unfamiliar.

"Put on your kep and come awa' doon the toon wi' me," she said to Erchie. "I hate gaun into some o' thae big shops mysel'."

"Then whit wye dae ye no' jist gang into the wee yins ye ken?" he asked her. "If ye're feared they'll eat ye in the big yins I wadna gang to them."

"Oh, that's a' very weel, but the wee yins havena the turnover," she explained. "Ye get things far fresher at this time o' the year doon the toon."

"I'll gang wi' ye, for I ken that if I didna gang they wad tak' a fair lend o' ye," Erchie agreed a last; "but mind, I'm no' gaun to stand lookin' in at baby-linen shop-windows or onything o' that sort.

Me bein' a public man in a kind o' wye, it disna dae."

"I'll no' ask ye to dae onything o' the kind, ye pridefu' auld thing ye," she promised, and off they set.

She wanted a pair of gloves for a favourite grand-daughter, an umbrella for a sister of Erchie's, who was a widow and poor, and something as a wedding-present for Duffy's fiancée.

There was scarcely a drapery warehouse in Argyle Street whose window did not attract her. Erchie never looked into any of them, but patiently stood apart on the edge of the pavement or walked slowly ahead.

"Come here and see this at seevenpence three-fardens," she entreated him.

"It's fine, a rale bargain, I wad tak' that." he replied, looking forward towards the window from afar off, and quite ignorant of what she alluded to, but determined not to be caught by any one, who knew him as waiter or beadle, looking into a shop-window full of the most delicate feminine mysteries of attire.

She went into the warehouse, while he walked on to the next shop—a cutler's—and looked intently in at the window of it, as if he were contemplating the purchase of a costly pocket-knife with five blades, a corkscrew, and an appliance popularly supposed to be for taking stones out of a horse's hoof. When he was joined by Jinnet, she had plainly begun to lose her nerve.

"I've got gloves," she said, "and a thing for Duffy's lass, but they're naither o' them whit I was wantin'."

"Of course they're no'," said Erchie. "Ye've got a grate consait o' yersel', if ye think a puir auld body like you can get exactly whit ye want in yin o' them warehooses wi' the big turnover ye aye talk aboot. Was it a peerie and a fiddle ye wanted that made ye tak' gloves?"

"Oh! dinna bother me, Erchie, I canna help it. The lassies that serve ye in there's that Englified and that smert that when they havena got whit I'm wantin' I jist aye tak' whit they can gie me."

"I've seen you in a big shop afore noo," said her husband, "and I ken fine the wye ye aye spile yersel' wi' them Englified smert yins. Ye gang forrit to the coonter as if ye were gaun to ask if they had ony windows to clean, or back-stairs to wash oot, and ye get red in the face and tak' yer money oot o' yer pocket to show ye have it, and ye laugh to the lassie as if ye kent her fine, and ye say, 'If you please' to her, or, 'Oh! it's a bother to ye.' That mak's the lassie see at yince ye're no' cless. She gets a' the mair Englified, lettin' on to hersel' she's the Dutchess o' Montrose, and can put the like o' you in your place wi' the least wee bit touch. That's no' the wye to dae it in a shop o' that kind. Ye should breenge up to the coonter, and cry 'Gloves!' as hard as Duffy cries 'Coals!' then sit doon withoot askin' on a chair and, wi' a gant noo and then, watch them puttin' oot gloves by the hunderwicht in front o' ye, and them a' in the shakers in case ye'll no' think they're smert enough.

"Dinna be blate. That's my advice to ye. Talk Englified yersel', and sniff wi' yer nose noo and then as if ye felt a nesty smell in the place, and run doon the goods like dirt. Never let your e'e rest on the folk that serve ye, unless they happen to hae a shabby tie on or a button aff somewhere. Glower at that, and it'll mak' them uncomfortable, and——"

"Ooh, that's a' richt, Erchie," said Jinnet, "ye'll hae to come into the next shop I gang to, and show me the wye."

"No fears o' me," said Erchie promptly; "I'm tellin' ye whit to dae, but I divna say I could dae't mysel'."

But when it came to the purchase of the umbrella he did go into the shop with her, and she got what she thought was a bargain, as well as the finest affability and courtesy from the gentleman who sold it.

"That's because I was wi' ye," said Erchie, when they came out.

"I daresay," she agreed; "there's aye some use for a man."

XXVIII

A BET ON BURNS

Duffy came round to Erchie's on Saturday night for the loan of a copy of Burns, which he knew the old man had on the shelves of what he called his chevalier and book-case. "I'm wantin' to learn a sang," said he, "for I'm gaun to the Haggis Club in the Mull o' Kintyre Vaults on Monday if I'm spared."

"Are ye, indeed!" said Erchie, drily. "Ye'll be takin' the new wife wi' ye?"

"No fears o' me," said Duffy. "Wha ever heard o' a wife at a Burns meetin'?"

"Oh! I divna ken onything aboot it," said Erchie; "I thocht maybe the weemen were gaun to thae things nooadays, though they didna go when I was young, and I thocht maybe you bein' sae lately mairried ye wanted to gie her a trate. It's a droll thing aboot Burns that though the weemen were sae ta'en up wi' him when he was livin', they're no' awfu' keen on him noo that he's deid. There'll be thoosands o' men hurrayin' Burns on Monday nicht in a' pairts o' the warld, and eatin' haggis till they're no weel, but I'll bate ye their wifes is no' there. No! There wifes is at hame mendin' their men's sox, and chairgin' the gazogene for the morn's mornin', when it'll be sair wanted. And ye're gaun to a Haggis Club, are ye? I didna ken ye were such a keen Burns hand."

"Me!" cried Duffy, "I'm jist daft for Burns. Fifty or mair o' the members tak' their coals frae me. Burns! Man, Erchie, I could gie ye Burns by the yaird—'Dark Lochnagar,' and 'The Flooers o' the Forest,' 'We're a' Noddin','' and 'Rollin' Hame to Bonnie Scotland'—

> 'Rollin' hame to Bonnie Scotland,
> Rollin' hame across the sea.'"

He sang the lines with gusto.

"Stop!" said Erchie, in alarm, "stop! There's nae deafenin' in thae ceilin's, and the folk abin 'll think I'm giein' Jinnet a leatherin'. Man! I didna think ye kent sae mony o' Rabbie's sangs. It's a credit to ye. I'm shair ye divna need ony book to learn affa."

"To tell ye the rale sets o't, Erchie," said Duffy, "it's a bate. There's a chap yonder at the coal hill thrieps doon my throat Burns didna write 'Dark Lochnagar' the wye I sing't, and I want to show him 't in the book."

"Hoo much is the bate?" said Erchie.

"Hauf-a-croon," said Duffy.

"Then sell yin o' yer horses and pay the money," said Erchie, "for ye've lost the bate. Burns had nae grudge against his countrymen. They did him nae hairm. He didna write 'Dark Lochnagar' the wye you sing it, for Burns never made his sangs wi' a saw. In fact, he never wrote 'Dark Lochnagar' at a'. It was put oot by anither firm in the same tred, ca'd Byron."

"My jove!" said Duffy, "I never kent that afore!"

"There's lots o' things ye never kent," said Erchie. "Seein' ye're gaun to eat haggis on Monday nicht, ye micht tell us whit ye ken, no' aboot Burn's sangs, but aboot Burns himself'."

"There was naething wrang wi' the chap," said Duffy, "if he just had stuck to his wark. When I'm sellin' coal I'm sellin' coal, and no' pentin' pictures. But there was Burns; if he happened to come on a moose's nest in the field when he was plewin', or see a flooer in his road when he was oot workin' at the hye, he wad stop the plew, or lay doon his rake, and tak' the efternoon aff to mak' a sang aboot the moose or the daisy."

"A', and jist wi' his least wee bit touch," said Erchie, admiringly. "He was great, that's whit he was."

"Maybe he was, but it spiled the wark. We wadna aloo that in the coal tred," said Duffy. "He didna ken what compeetition was. I've seen things in my ain tred a knacky chap could mak' a fine sang aboot if he was jist lettin' himsel' go."

"Then for mercy's sake aye keep a grip o' yersel'," said Erchie. "Mind ye hae a wife dependin' on ye!"

"And then," said Duffy, "he was a bit o' the la-di-da. There's naething o' the la-di-da aboot me."

"There is not!" admitted Erchie, frankly.

"But Burns, although he was a plewman to tred, went aboot wi' a di'mond ring spilin' folks' windows. If he saw a clean pane o' gless he never lost the chance o' writin' a bit verse on't wi' his di'mond ring. It was gey chawin' to the folk the windows belanged to' but Burns never cared sae lang's he let them see he had a rale di'mond ring that wad scratch gless."

"It was the fashion at the time, Duffy," said Erchie. "Nooadays when a poet has an idea for twa lines he keeps it under the bed till it sproots into a hale poem, and then he sends it to a magazine, and buys his wife, or somebody else's a di'mond ring wi' whit he gets for't. Writin' on window-panes is no' the go ony langer. It's oot o' date."

"But I'm no' runnin' doon the chap," said Duffy. "Only I aye thocht it was him that wrote 'Dark Lochnagar.' Are ye shair it wasna?"

Erchie nodded. "Nor 'Rollin' Hame to Bonnie Scotland' either. He was far ower busy writin' sangs aboot the Marys, and the Jeans, and the Peggys at the time to write aboot ony o' yer 'Dark Lochnagars.'"

"So he was," admitted Duffy. "Yon's a rare yin aboot Mary—

'Kind, kind, and gentle is she—
. . . kind is my Mary,
The tender blossom on the tree
Is half sae sweet as Mary.'"

"Calm yersel', Duffy," said Erchie, in dramatic alarm. "I'm no deaf."

"That was written aboot 'Hielan' Mary,'" said Duffy. "He met her at Dunoon the Fair Week, and I've seen her monument."

"It's yonder as nate's ye like," said Erchie. "Faith! it's you that's weel up in Burns, Duffy."

"Oh! I'm no' that faur back in my history," said Duffy, quite pleased with himself. "But I could hae sworn it was him that put thegither 'Rollin' Hame to Bonnie Scotland', it's his style. He micht be rollin', but he aye got hame. He was a gey wild chap, Burns."

"I'm no' denyin't, Duffy," said Erchie. "But he hadna ony o' the blessin's we have in oor time to keep him tame. There was nae Free Leebrary to provide him wi' books to keep him in the hoose at nicht, nae Good Templar Lodges to help him in keepin' clear o' the horrors o' drink, and Poosy Nancy's public-hoose didna shut at ten o'clock, nor even eleeven. If Burns had thae advantages, there's nae sayin' whit he micht hae risen to. Perhaps he micht hae become an M.P., and dee'd wi' money in the bank."

"Och! there's worse than Burns," said Duffy. "I was gey throughither mysel' when I was a young chap."

"Ah! but ye couldna hae been that awfu' bad, for ye never made ony poetry."

"I never tried," said Duffy, "I was the youngest o' nine, and I was put oot to wark early. So there wisna time for me to try and be fancy in ony wye. But a gey wild chap, Burns!"

"Maybe no' that awfu' wild," said Erchie. "Ye're aye harpin' on the wild. Burns was like a man takin' a daunder oot in a country road on a fine nicht. He kept his een sae much on the stars that sometimes he tripped in the sheuch. If it was the like o' you and me, Duffy, we wad be keepin' oor e'e a' the time on the road at oor feet to see if onybody hadna dropped onything, and there wad be nae fears o' us fa'in in the sheuch. Except for his habit o' makin' sangs when he micht be makin' money, Burns wasna very different frae the rest o' us. There was ae thing aboot him—he aye payed his way, and never forgot his freen's. He had a warm hert."

"Man, ye should be doon at the Mull o' Kintyre Vaults Haggis Club on Monday and propose the toast," said Duffy, admiringly.

"I'm better whaur I am," said Erchie; "the best Burns Club a man can hae 's a weel-thumbed copy o' the poems on his chevalier and book-case, and a wife that can sing 'Ye Banks and Braes' like oor Jinnet."

XXIX

THE PRODIGAL'S RETURN

A sailor-man with a thick black beard, and all his belongings apparently on his back; for the dunnage-bag he carried was so poorly stuffed it could have held little more than a pair of sea-boots, went into Erchie's close one afternoon, and slowly climbed the stair. He put the bag at his feet when he came to Erchie's door with "MacPherson" on the name-plate, scratched his head, hitched his waist-belt once or twice, and seemed in a mood to turn and flee rather than to ring or knock. At last he faintly tugged the bell-pull, and leaned against the door-post with the air of one who expected he might have some parley before getting admittance.

There was a step in the lobby, and Erchie himself in his shirt-sleeves came to the door.

"We're no' for onything the day," said he. "We have a sewin'-machine already, and we're a' in the Prudential Insurance, and the staircase windows were cleaned on Setturday, and——"

"Faither," said the sailor-man, "do ye no' ken me?"

Erchie came closer and looked at the bearded face, and put his hand trembling upon the young man's shoulder.

"Willie!" said he. "Willie!" he repeated. "Man, ye're sair needin' shavin'." He shook his son, and "O, Willie," said he, "whit 'll yer mither say? I suppose if I was the rale thing mysel', I should kill the fatted calf or start the greetin. But as shair's death we havena kept a calf in this hoose since ye left it yoursel', and I was never yin o' the greetin' kind. My goodness! Willie!"

He was so bewildered he forgot his visitor stood on the door-mat, until Willie lifted his dunnage-bag, and then he urged him into the kitchen.

"Where's—where's mother?" said the sailor.

"She micht be deid and in her grave for you," said his father; "but she's no'. She's doon at Lindsay the grocer's for a loaf. Oh, ye rogue! ye rogue! Whit 'll she say to ye? Seeven years, come the fifth o' June! Oh, ye're awfu' needin' shavin'. I hope—I hope the health's fine?"

"Fine," said Willie, and sat in a chair uneasily, like a stranger.

"And whaur in a' the warld did ye come frae?" said his father, putting the kettle on the fire. They had not even shaken hands.

"China and roond aboot there," said the son.

125

"China!" said his father. "And hoo did ye leave them a' in China? They're throng at the war there the noo, I see. I hope ye werena hurted."

"No, nor hurted," said Willie. "I hope ye're fine yersel'. And mother?"

"Me!" said Erchie. "Jist a fair gladiator! Divna ken my ain strength, and can eat onything, jist like a connoshoor. As for yer mother, she's wonderfu'; a wee frail, but aye able to dae her turns. She'll be the gled wumman this—— Whit I mean to say is, ye should get a reg'lar leatherin' for your cairry-on. If I hadna my rheumatism in my shoother gey bad, I wad tak' a stick to ye. I'm pretty wild at ye, mind I'm tellin' ye. Whit dae ye think o' yersel', to gang awa' and no' write us for seeven years?"

"No' an awfu' lot," said the son.

"That's hopeful," said his father. "I'm gled ye're no' puttin' the blame on us. And I'm gled ye havena ony brass buttons on your claes."

"Brass buttons?" said Willie.

"Ay! When your mother was wearyin' to hear frae ye, I used to be tellin' her that ye were likely a mate, or a purser, or something o' that sort, and that busy in foreign pairts liftin' the tickets in the fore saloon, where the dram's cheaper and maist o' the passengers go, that ye hadna time to write. Yince I took her doon to the docks and showed her a big ship gaun awa' to Australia, wi' the Captain on the tap flet, ca'in a handle and roarin' 'Let go that gangway!' and 'Nae smokin' abaft the funnel!' and she was as pleased as onything to see't. Ever since then she thinks o' her son Willie as a chap wi' brass buttons ca'in a handle the same as he was a tramway driver, and that busy he hadna time to write. I'm gled ye havena brass buttons," concluded Erchie, looking at his rather shabbily clothed scion. "It's mair to your credit that ye were jist a fool and no' a rascal."

"Man, ye're jist as great a caution as ever," said Willie, with the sincerest admiration.

"Duffy the coal-man tellt me he saw ye yince doon aboot the Broomielaw," said Erchie. "It was three years ago. I daursay ye were ower throng at the time to come up and see your mither and me. It's a guid wye up here frae the Broomielaw. It costs a penny on the skoosh car. Or maybe it was a wet day."

Willie's face got red. "It wasna only yince I was at the

Broomielaw," he said. "I've been in Gleska four times since I left it."

"Were ye indeed?" said his father. "Weel, weel, it was rale considerate o' ye no' to bother your auld mither and me. I'll wager ye werena needin' ony money."

"I was needin' money gey bad every time," said the son. "I aye had some when I landed, but it never got past the Broomielaw wi' me. And that's the wye I never cam near ye. I was ashamed, as shair's death. Every time I was in the Clyde I cam up here at nicht, or to the auld hoose afore ye flitted, and looked at the close or went roond to the back coort and looked at the kitchen window."

"It's a good thing I didna see ye there, or I wad maybe hae gien ye a clourin'."

"I wad hae liked it fine if ye had," said the young man. "A clourin' was the very thing I was needin', and I kent it mysel'. I was an awfu' fool, faither."

"That's jist whit ye were," Erchie admitted. "It's a lingerin' disease, and that's the warst o't. I hope ye'll maybe get ower't."

"If I didna think I had got ower't I wadna hae been here the nicht," said the son. "I'll warrant ye'll no' hae to complain o' me again."

Erchie took his hand. "Willie," said he, "gie me your thoomb on that. I ken the MacPhersons, if their mind's made up, and I think ye're auld enough noo to try your hand at sense. It'll no' hurt ye. Willie, Willie, it wasna mysel' I worried aboot thae seeven years, nor you either. For I kent fine the prodigal wad come back, if it was only to see if his faither de'ed and left him onything. The prodigal son! Awfu' needin' a shave! Your mither'll be the prood wumman this nicht."

Before Jinnet had come back from the grocer's Erchie put his son into the parlour, so that the returned wanderer might not too abruptly confront his mother. She suspected nothing for a little, going about her ordinary offices in the kitchen till something fidgety in her husband's appearance directed her more close attention to him, and there was seen then an elation in his countenance that made her ask him what the matter was.

"Ye're awfu' joco," said he. "Are ye plannin' some baur for Duffy?"

"Not me," said Erchie. "I'm jist wearyin' for my tea. And, by the wye, Jinnet," he added, "ye micht put doon anither cup for a frien' o' mine I'm expectin' frae abroad."

"Frae abroad!" cried Jinnet, turning pale. "Ye havena heard onything o'—o'——"

"Have I no'?" said Erchie. "There's a chap in the room at this meenute that wad be awfu' like Willie if he had a clean shave."

Ten minutes later Erchie joined his wife and Willie in the room. The dunnage-bag was being emptied before Jinnet by a son who was anxious to make the most of his gifts from foreign parts, though painfully conscious of their value.

"Oh, whit braw shells!" cried his mither. "Jist the very thing I was needin' for the mantelpiece. The Carmichaels say wally dugs is no' the go noo at a'. It was rale thochtfu' o' ye to tak' them a' the wye frae abroad for me."

"And here a song folio and a pund o' sweet tobacco for you, faither," said Willie.

Erchie took them in his hand. "Man, that's the very thing," said he. "If 'Dark Lochnagar's' in't, I'll be upside wi' Duffy."

"Whit's this?" asked Jinnet, as the sailor brought forth for her a bottle containing some dark thick fluid.

"Riga balsam,—whit the sailors use for sair hands," said Willie.

"Oh, it's the very thing Erchie used to say ye wad bring back when ye cam," cried Jinnet in delight. "It'll be awfu' useful. I'm almost vext I havena onything sair aboot me the day."

"No' even a sair hert," said Erchie, and the son looked contritely at his mother."